Walking the Hudson

Also by Cy A Adler

Walking by Waters: NY–NJ and Hudson Shorewalking Photos

Walking Manhattan's Rim: The Great Saunter

Ecological Fantasies: Death from Falling Watermelons

The Queer Dutchman

Wholly Mother Jones, a play with music

Walking the Hudson

From the Battery to Bear Mountain

The First Guide to Walking the First 56 Miles of the
Proposed Hudson River Shore Trail

Cy A Adler

With a foreword by Pete Seeger

Countryman Press
Woodstock, Vermont

Walking the Hudson
978-0-88150-946-5

Interior photos by the author unless otherwise specified
Book design and composition by Caroline Rufo
Maps by Erin Greb Cartography, ©The Countryman Press

Published by The Countryman Press, P.O. Box 748, Woodstock, VT 05091

Distributed by W.W. Norton & Company, Inc., 500 Fifth Avenue, New York, NY 10110

Printed in the United States of America

10 9 8 7 6 5 4 3 2 1

To Moses, Xenophon, Wordsworth,
Coleridge, Jane Austen, Audubon, Thoreau,
John Muir, and Mao Tse-Tung
—strong-legged walkers all

Collecting things is good; shorewalking is better.

—a Shorewalker's motto

CONTENTS

The first edition of this book was independently published by Green Eagle Press in 1997. It sold out. In 1839, Henry Thoreau, a guy who loved nature, sailed for a week with his brother in a homemade boat on the Concord and Merrimack rivers. His account of the voyage, published at his own expense in 1849, sold 215 copies. This venture put him in debt for several years.

FOREWORD

I love the title BATT TO BEAR!
For folks who like walking from here to there,
Cy Adler is my kind of environment man,
He takes a situation right in hand.
"Suburbanite, no longer nature mar:
If you want to save the planet,
move to towns where you don't need a car."

Cy has walked more than 10,000 miles of waterfront, mostly on weekends with Shorewalkers, the New York City–based hiking club. He has explored the Jersey and Long Island Atlantic shore; the Bronx, Arthur, and other kills; and the mighty Gowanus as well as the Hudson River. Every city should have a group like Shorewalkers.

But right now, look into this book. It's the first chapter in the creation of the 300-mile Hudson River Shore Trail.

Get out those hiking shoes.

Pete Seeger

Beacon, New York

1997

Author's note: Pete has been very supportive of this revised edition as well.

Preface: Get Lost

Consider yourself lucky should you get lost walking along the Hudson River shore. *Walking the Hudson* will give you enough information to get lost—or to find a road that may eventually lead you home. Getting lost assures you of seeing something new, something you did not know was there. Along this Queen of Rivers, sharp-eyed seekers and ramblers will find many natural and man-made wonders.

If you get lost on the Hudson River Shore Trail, dogs and ticks may attack you; fend them off. Millionaires may order you off estates they claim are theirs. Smile and hum Woody Guthrie's famous song: "As I went walking, I saw a sign there / . . . it said 'private property.' / But on the other side it didn't say nothin' / That side was made for you and me." Railway dicks may try to dissuade you should you wander along railroad rights-of-way. Smile as you leave and point out that railroads are public charters, and that local Hudson River residents walk along (not on) the tracks all the time.

You cannot go wrong if you keep your senses tuned to nature and the flow of the Hudson. Keep walking.

Cy A Adler

New York Island

2012

ACKNOWLEDGMENTS

This guide is the result of the efforts of many dedicated people to preserve the Hudson River shore and to allow more people to enjoy the river. I hope this book will provide a way for people to walk on the edge of one of the world's most beautiful waterways—a wide estuarine river within hailing distance of the New York–New Jersey metro area.

Foot explorers who helped scout the Hudson River Shore Trail (HRST) include Minor Bishop, Rachel Donner, Ted Gabay, Jag Gulati, Ursula Hahn, Buddy Levine, Gordon Linzner, and Dorothy Lourdou—all of whom have given me helpful comments. I am most grateful. During the work week they are an architect, an English teacher, an administrator, a retired garment worker, a molecular bio-researcher, a novelist, an engineer, and a dance librarian. On weekends this intrepid crew has walked in snow and in 95-degree weather along the Hudson's shores, exploring inlets, hamlets, rocks, sand, and both green and gray paths so that others may follow. These bipeds are members of Shorewalkers, a not-for-profit environmental and walking group founded in 1982.

For this revised edition, I would like to thank Susannah Black, Peter Nekola, Ed Liebowitz, Joe Halstead, Christine Yost, and Ginger Ray. I would also like to thank my editors at Countryman Press, Lisa Sacks and Caitlin Martin.

The Hudson River Shore Trail is the proposed 330-mile footpath along the river outlined in the *New York Times* in my September 1, 1984, Op-Ed piece: "For Hudsonophiles, a Long, Long Trail." A vast hodgepodge of data and Hudson impressions have accumulated in my files since the 1980s, and without the assistance of Jewel Daniel, a native of St. Kitts, this book would not have been assembled and typed. I am most grateful for her youthful energy and talent.

In addition, I would like to thank long-term supporters of the

▶ *Part of the Great Saunter 2011, walkers head north along the Hudson River around West 82nd Street.*

Christine Yost

Shorewalkers' efforts to create the 330-mile HRST. Since 1984 these farsighted environmentalists have included, among others, Mrs. Willis Reese; Mrs. George W. Perkins; Ms. Evelyn Lauder; William L. Frost; Logan Fulrath Jr.; Pete Seeger; legislators and former legislators Maurice Hinchey, Ed Sullivan, and Franz Leichter; the Mertz-Gilmore Foundation; and the REI Foundation.

Lastly, thanks to the New York State Department of Environmental Conservation for help in producing the four-color map of the Batt to Bear Trail that can be found on www.shorewalkers.org, as well as Con Edison for support of the Great Saunter, which traverses 11 miles of the Batt to Bear Trail along the Hudson River.

INTRODUCTION

The Hudson River Shore Trail (HRST) from the Battery to the Adirondacks will be the living spine of the Hudson River greenway now being pieced together along the Hudson in New York and New Jersey. The greenway will protect open space along the shores, provide access to the water, and allow citizens healthful recreation at small cost. Many fragments of the route already exist in parks, unused railroad rights-of-way, secondary river roads, and promenades. Hundreds of citizens in river communities are involved in efforts to build parts of the trail in their areas. I see this continuous hiking path as a gateway to recreational opportunities for coming generations. It will also inhibit land speculators eager to condominiumize these beautiful riverbanks.

More than 4 million people a year are likely to use the HRST when it is strung together. This estimate is based on current usage of the Appalachian Trail (AT). The mountainous,

◀ *Heading west over the George Washington Bridge to the Jersey Palisades.*

2,144-mile-long AT is less accessible to most Americans than the HRST and less conducive to fishing or swimming. The Appalachian Trail Conference, the volunteer group that maintains the AT through the hills of 14 states, estimates 3 million hikers walk the trail annually. Most are local day-trippers. About 1,700 "end-to-enders" annually try for the long haul; fewer than 300 complete it. Most of the people who will walk along the HRST will be day-trippers from communities such as Bayonne, the Bronx, Nyack, Newburgh, Albany, and the Adirondacks.

Starting at the mouth of the Hudson at the south end of Manhattan, the trail leads north past skyscrapers and piers; through Riverside, Battery, Rockefeller, Hudson River, Fort Washington, Riverbank, and other city parks; and to the George Washington Bridge (GWB). On November 25, 1984, the Shorewalkers, an environmental and outdoors group, joined by more than 50 "Hudsonophiles," designated the leg from the Battery to the Little Red Lighthouse as part of the Hudson River Shore Trail with a ceremonial white sock that had been walked along Lake Tear-of-the-Clouds, over 4,000 feet high on the slopes of Mount Marcy in the Adirondacks. This lake is commonly thought of as the source of the Hudson. The old sock, along with a deceased gerbil named Gerb, was buried in an old shoebox near the Little Red Lighthouse beneath the bridge, symbolizing the mixing of waters from both ends of the river. This area has since been paved over. I assume both the sock and Gerb lie below.

North of the lighthouse the trail crosses the GWB from Washington Heights into Fort Lee, New Jersey, and then heads north beneath the Palisades. Then it winds through state parks and along an abandoned railroad right-of-way from Nyack to Piermont on the way to Bear Mountain. North of the Bear Mountain Bridge the trail is not established. In theory it will go through old towns, past farms, through meadows and wetlands, and along train tracks to Albany; then on to Glens Falls; and finally into the deep woods of the Adirondacks and to

Lake Henderson. Lake Henderson is a few miles from Lake Tear-of-the-Clouds on Mount Marcy. We have moved the end point slightly in deference to Adirondack conservationists, some of whom feel the Lake Tear area is already overused.

Using this guide, the diligent shorewalker can walk along a mighty body of moving water. Atlantic tides flow into New York Bay, pulled by the gravitational force of the moon and sun. From upper New York Bay, the salt waters pulse twice a day between the Palisades to the west and the New York City boroughs of Manhattan and the Bronx to the east. North of the city, past Yonkers, the river widens into the Tappan Zee. It narrows again north of Nyack, then widens to more than 3.5 miles at Haverstraw Bay, its widest expanse. North, and on either side of the bay, are the Hudson Highlands, a grand and hilly stretch where the massive fortress of West Point overlooks the deepest part of the river—some 200 feet—scoured out by the fast-moving current.

Farther upriver, between Beacon/Newburgh and Poughkeepsie, the tidal estuary loses most of its salt and turns into a tidal river. Fresh water moving downstream still feels the tidal force; the tidal bore moves north, past Kingston on the west bank and the town of Hudson on the east bank, another 50 miles to Albany. A few miles north of Albany, the Atlantic tide nudges against the dam at Troy twice a day.

The federal dam at Troy divides the lower Hudson estuarine basin from the meandering 150 miles of stream in the Adirondack Mountains. The fast-rising northern half of the Hudson flows through forests past the small towns of Mechanicsville, Fort Edward, Glens Falls, and tiny Adirondack communities nestled amid the green woods.

Hundreds of springs and creeks feed the main Hudson stream, which starts more than 4,300 feet above sea level on Mount Marcy. The Hudson River is about 315 miles long. If and when walking paths along both riverbanks are completed, these shore trails should measure more than 660 miles due to the twisting of the river, and routes blocked by power plants and private owners—the vicissitudes of nature tempered by the efforts of humankind.

East of the Hudson River lie the border counties of eastern New York State, the Berkshire Mountains of New England, and the Taconic Range, which extends south through Westchester and the Bronx. Spuyten Duyvil Creek, the Croton River, Wappinger's Creek, and the Fishkill are a few of the Hudson's eastern tributaries. From the west flow the mighty Mohawk River, the Roundout, the Catskill, the Walkill, and some 60 other creeks and rivulets. Tidal waters from Newark Bay, into which pour the Hackensack and Passaic rivers, mix with the tidal flow of the estuarine Hudson near its mouth. The Hudson River ecosystem is an extremely rich, productive, and complex brew. Shore walkways that would remain forever green would help to protect this great stream from wanton destruction.

The south Hudson section, from the mouth of the river at the Battery to Bear Mountain Bridge, a distance of about 56 miles, is the subject of this guide.

The mid-Hudson section, from Bear Mountain to the Troy Dam, is about 100 miles passing orchards, great estates, and small towns nestled between the Hudson highlands and the water.

The north Hudson section, from Troy to the headwaters of the Hudson near Lake Henderson and Lake Tear-of-the-Clouds, is a wilder reach of about 150 miles.

Of these three major sections, Shorewalkers have scouted the entire south section, which can be walked in its entirety. We have also wandered over many sections of the mid- and northern Hudson sections. We have walked the diverse, beautiful south section path, varied and continuous all the way with pleasures for the eye and the mouth as well as the legs. We trust that in our lifetime a few miles of the route can be rerouted around several obstructions.

In the mid-Hudson section, progress has been made in building trails and access points along the river through the communities on the eastern shore. Several local riverine residents are fearful that New York State will impose a "greenway" plan upon them, which will reduce the value of their land. From 1980 to 2008, speculation drove up the price of Hudson Valley land. The financial real estate bubble may have given local residents a distorted image of the value of their riverside property. The economic downturn of 2008 appears to be cooling speculative real estate frenzies and fantasies. We trust this will benefit the environment along the river.

In the north Hudson section, from Troy to Mount Marcy, one now can walk almost the entire length using existing secondary river roads and nonfunctioning railroad rights-of-way. In 1990 Tom Monroe of the N.Y.S. Department of Environmental Conservation drew a map for a Shorewalkers-sponsored Symposium entitled *Linking up the Hudson River Shore Trail,* in which he indicated the Northern Basin's "areas of difficulty." Tom's map clearly showed that most of the Adirondack section was accessible to walkers. An HRST-Adirondack trail here will benefit the river, local communities who depend on tourism, and our children for coming generations. The symposium, which took place at the Hudson River Museum in Yonkers, brought together park lovers, park officials, and trail advocates to help plan and promote greenways along the river.

I am most familiar with the south Hudson section of the HRST and will try to describe it in this book. The Battery to Bear Mountain (Batt to Bear) Trail is the one most likely to be used by the 25 million New Jersey–New York residents of the metropolitan area; by the residents of Putnam, Rockland, Westchester, and Orange counties; and by visitors and tourists.

For Hudsonophiles, A Long, Long Trail

New York Times, September 1, 1984

By Cyrus A Adler

Two years ago, while I was leading a group through Riverside Park, along the Hudson River, to the Irish bars of Inwood, someone said to me: "It would be great if people could hike all the way to where the river rises." Since then, members of my group and I have been talking to hikers and bikers, walkers and talkers, bureaucrats, state legislators and assorted river rats — Hudsonophiles all — about putting together a 330-mile hiking path along the shores of the Hudson.

While most have encouraged our effort, they have also warned of the difficulty of beating the land-grabbers to the valuable stretches of real estate that the path would cover. We will have to move quickly, for many of the old estates held by religious groups and private families are too expensive for their owners to maintain. And there is plenty of money available to finance development: More than 50 river-front projects have been proposed within the past year, most of them condominums that would exclude the public from the waterfront.

The Hudson trail would start at the Hudson's mouth at the Battery in Manhattan, go north past piers and skyscrapers, through Riverside Park to the George Washington Bridge.

Putting together a hiking path

After crossing the big bridge to Fort Lee, N.J., the trail would wind beneath Palisade cliffs, through parks, old brick towns, fields of apple and grape, meadows and wetlands, to Albany. Beyond Glens Falls, villages shrink to outposts first visited by Indians. From Tahawus, in the Adirondacks, the hiker must snake through deep forests and around Lakes Jimmy and Sally to the source of the Hudson, Lake Tear of the Clouds, high on the flank of New York's tallest peak, Mount Marcy. A hiker could traverse the Hudson trail in two to four weeks.

The Hudson River shore trail would insure citizens' access to some of America's most beautiful scenery before it is condominiumized and lost forever. It would allow upstaters to get better acquainted with downstaters, New Yorkers with Jerseyites. The trail would be a boon to birders, joggers, race walkers and nature lovers — if we can get it built.

Of the trail's estimated 330 miles, I would guess that more than 100 miles now exist in bits and pieces: I have walked stretches along the lower reaches of the Hudson, near West Point, Cold Spring, New Hamburg and Hyde Park. Other stretches of trail wind through state parks and cities — New York, Albany and Troy come to mind. With time and support, we can explore the virgin sections, connect them with existing legs, obtain easements, mark the trails, arrange for maintenance and tie them together into one glorious green walkway.

The Hudson trail would be a tribute to man's need for nature and for the blue water from which life sprang. In our mechanized, noisy age, we need solitude and the chance to sample wildness once in a while. Hikers could camp in parks along the river or stop in small hotels.

The proposed Hudson River shore trail would serve the interests of millions of people by providing recreation for coming generations and inhibiting speculators eager to corrupt the still beautiful river banks. With the help of the state government in obtaining rights of way, dedicated volunteers could blaze a trail at very little cost.

Money could be raised in part from the state and from the Federal Government, which passed the National

To assemble 330 miles is an uphill effort

Trail Systems Act in 1968 to encourage the building of outdoor trails. (Regrettably, the present Administration hasn't had much use for the act.) The rest could be raised from private sources, perhaps with the promise of placing milestones designed by local artists in recognition of major patrons and contributors.

During the past 20 years, the 2,000-mile Appalachian Trail has been reconstructed, the 210-mile Long Path to the Catskills has been put together and the 880-mile Potomac National Heritage Trail has slowly taken shape. The Potomac trail, which runs on both sides of the river and goes through Washington D.C., is similar in some ways to our proposed Hudson trail.

In many states, new hiking trails are being pieced together leg-by-leg, foot-by-foot and maintained by volunteers — such as those who belong to the 60 local hiking clubs that support the venerable New York-New Jersey Trail Conference. Joining these long nature trails, the Hudson River shore trail would be a unique pathway for our friends and those who follow. □

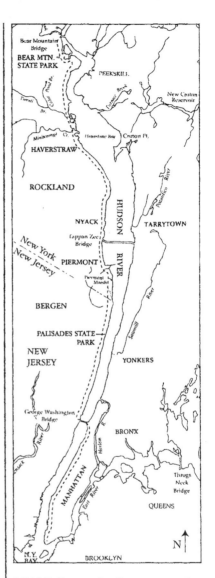

SCALE: From the Battery to the George Washington Bridge is about 12 miles.

We divide the Batt to Bear Trail into 11 segments or legs:

LEG 1:   The Battery to West 42nd Street—4.5 miles

LEG 2:   West 42nd Street to 125th Street—4.2 miles

LEG 3:   125th Street to the Little Red Lighthouse—3 miles

LEG 4:   The Little Red Lighthouse to Fort Lee—2 miles

LEG 5:   Fort Lee to Alpine—7 miles

LEG 6:   Alpine to the State Line—4–5 miles

LEG 7:   State Line to Piermont—3 miles

LEG 8:   Piermont to Nyack—3 miles

LEG 9:   Nyack to Haverstraw—9.5 miles

LEG 10:   Haverstraw to Tomkins Cove—5–6 miles

LEG 11:   Tomkins Cove to Bear Mountain—5–6 miles

Legs 1, 2, and 3 are to the east of the Hudson; legs 5 through 11 are to the west. We hope to extend the walk on the New Jersey side from Liberty Park to the George Washington Bridge as Hudson greenways expand.

I leave further development of the complete Hudson River Shore Trail to others. Keep walking.

Cheers,

Cy Adler

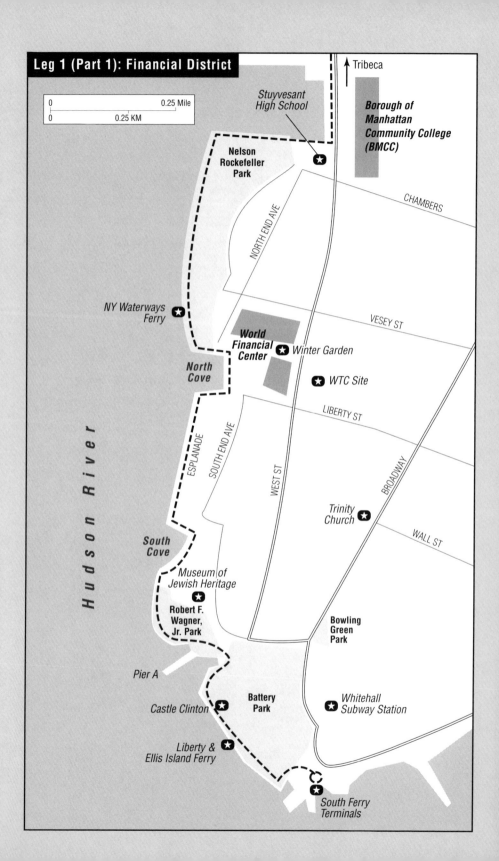

Leg 1 (Part 1): Financial District

0   0.25 Mile
0   0.25 KM

Tribeca

Stuyvesant High School

Borough of Manhattan Community College (BMCC)

Nelson Rockefeller Park

CHAMBERS

NORTH END AVE

NY Waterways Ferry

VESEY ST

World Financial Center

Winter Garden

WTC Site

North Cove

LIBERTY ST

ESPLANADE

SOUTH END AVE

WEST ST

BROADWAY

Trinity Church

WALL ST

South Cove

Hudson River

Museum of Jewish Heritage

Robert F. Wagner, Jr. Park

Bowling Green Park

Pier A

Castle Clinton

Battery Park

Whitehall Subway Station

Liberty & Ellis Island Ferry

South Ferry Terminals

LEG 1

THE BATTERY TO WEST 42ND STREET

ABOUT 4.5 MILES OF VARIED WATERFRONT

You do not complain to a beautiful morning.

—Walter Teller

The Hudson River Shore Trail begins at South Ferry, Battery Park, the southernmost tip of Manhattan Island. The long walk to the Hudson's source high on Mount Marcy begins surrounded by salt water at the Staten Island Ferry Terminal, where egg-shaped ferries depart for Staten Island to the south.

Walk north along the wide promenade in man-made Battery Park. The Dutch have a saying: "God made the world, but the Dutch made Holland." God also made New York Island, but New Yorkers have increased its area by another third by filling in the shallows along

◀ *The coastline of legs 1 and 2, as seen from the George Washington Bridge in 2011*

its shores. The path to the George Washington Bridge, about 11 miles north, a varied, historical, and beautiful trek, is almost entirely on human-made land.

Twenty-three-acre Battery Park gets its name from a row of guns that the Dutch, in the 17th century, placed along the original shore, which was situated inland of the present State Street. This charming, much-used park, which in 2010 hosted more than 4 million visitors, was built entirely on landfill. Circular Castle Clinton was constructed between 1807 and 1811, 300 feet offshore. It

Christine Yost

▲ *Shorewalkers walking north on the Batt to Bear Trail in the Battery Park area*

was one of three forts in the defense network of New York Harbor during the War of 1812. The British did not visit our city during that war, burning down Washington, DC, instead.

▼ *Main gate, Castle Clinton in Battery Park, New York City.*

Wikimedia Commons/Photo from the Historic American Buildings Survey (HABS)

Castle Clinton National Monument (212-344-7220; www.nps.gov/cacl) houses a historical museum and is part of the U.S. National Park System. After 1812 it was a performing arts stadium where Lafayette was welcomed in 1824, and in 1850, under the sponsorship of P. T. Barnum, Jenny Lind sang here. In 1855, renamed Castle Garden, it became the country's chief immigration depot, where Irish immigrants were recruited to fight in the Civil War. Here landed Italians, who moved into the flats of Mulberry Bend, followed by Jews escaping the horrors of late-19th-century Europe. From 1855 to 1890 some 8 million people entered the United States via the Castle Garden station. From 1896 to 1942, the station housed the city's main aquarium. In 1942, it was demolished. (The Coney Island Aquarium was built in 1957.)

▲ *19th-century stereoscopic card image of the Hudson Railroad, ca.1855–1930*   Wikimedia Commons

Two major highways tunnel beneath Battery Park. Their air vents are barely noticeable, and no noise from the traffic of the Brooklyn Battery Tunnel or the South Street–West Street connection mars the pleasant park ambience. Battery Park is an excellent reminder that, from civic and environmental viewpoints, the best thing to do with roadways in cities is to bury them! Automotive traffic is a major cause of urban air pollution, noise, and violent deaths in most of our cities. Putting autos in tunnels makes good civic and environmental sense.

The opening of the Erie Canal in 1825 brought barges of wheat and corn and cement and wood from the Great Lakes through to New York City piers, where these products were used, transplanted, or transported to the world. Railroad tracks laid parallel to the Hudson River brought passengers and cargo from inland America to New York City faster than the barges.

Nineteenth-century lower Manhattan was "belted round by wharves as Indian Isles by coral reefs," wrote Herman Melville in the opening lines of Moby Dick; "commerce surrounds it with its surf." The bustling Hudson and East River waterfronts secured New York's position as the preeminent American city. Ship commerce was the city's largest source of employment. Shipping began to fade in the 1930s as airplanes lured away foreign-bound passengers and cargo. After 1950, the Container Revolution forced ship terminals to be located near large uplands. Abandoned New York waterfront rotted in neglect, piers fell apart, and underutilized rail lines rusted and went to seed. New automotive bridges and tunnels hastened the decline of the passenger and freight ferries. The city attempted piece-meal to convert its waterfront piecemeal to other uses, but that's another story.

Yet the human appeal of Manhattan's watery edge has changed little

▼ *Statue of Liberty at dusk, as seen from Battery Park,*
Lower Manhattan

Wikimedia Commons/A.jo

since Melville stalked this island's coast in the 19th century and wrote that here came: "Men fixed in ocean reveries . . . landsmen: on weekdays pent up in lathe and plaster—tied to counters, nailed to benches, clinched to desks. Nothing will content them but the extreme limit of the land. They must get just as nigh the water as they possibly can without falling in. And there they stand. Inlanders all, they come from lanes and alleys, streets and avenues—north, east, south, and west. Yet here they all unite."

Several famous islands lapped by the salt tides in the Upper Bay of New York Harbor are visible from the Battery Park promenade. To the west, hugging the Jersey shore, are Ellis and Liberty islands. Ellis Island was 3 acres in size when used in the 1600s by the Mohegan Indians as an oyster fishery ground. Now it is 27 acres with three large buildings. It is most widely known as the "gateway" to the United States—more than 12 million immigrants from Europe, Africa, and Asia passed through the island between 1892 and 1954. One out of four Americans alive today is descended from that eager flow of humanity. Refurbished as an impressive and moving national museum (at a cost of $163 million) in the 1980s, Ellis Island (212-313-3200; www.ellisisland.org) can be reached by a 10-minute boat ride from the Battery Park promenade.

South of Ellis Island on Liberty Island stands the lady with the flame. Formerly Bedloe's Island (after the Bedloe family), Liberty Island was purchased by the state of New York in 1796. The state ceded it to the federal government in 1800 for the construction of Fort Wood, which was part of the harbor defenses for the War of 1812. The 30-foot-high, star-shaped fort wall is now the massive base for Auguste Bartholdi's 150-foot Statue of Liberty. In her left hand she holds a tablet inscribed with the date July 4, 1776. This monumental symbol of American openness and liberty was dedicated by President Grover Cleveland on October 28, 1886.

Southeast of Liberty Island lies Governors Island, which houses the Urban Assembly New York Harbor School, a public high school focused on maritime skills and the environmental restoration of the harbor. The island, built almost entirely of fill, is a part of Manhattan. It has been host to a Coast Guard base, a race track and summer resort, a prisoner-of-war camp,

Wikimedia Commons/John Hill

▲ *New York, from Governors Island. No. 20 of the Hudson River Portfolio. Published by Henry I. Megarey, New York.*

and a troop embarkation point. Castle William, a massive masonry bastion on the island, stood sentry over New York Harbor during the War of 1812, a deterrent to a possible attack by the British fleet. The inner-harbor forts soon became obsolete as the range of naval guns increased. On the island is Manhattan's only golf course. Now owned by the people of New York City, Governors Island attracts thousands of visitors in the summer months to bike around, examine Castle William, or just stroll and gawk at the seascape of New York Harbor.

South of South Ferry, the Verrazano Bridge's tall towers suspend a roadway connecting Brooklyn and Staten Island. Its span is 4,280 feet, the longest in the United States. Built by Robert Moses's Triboro Bridge and Tunnel Authority, it was opened in 1964 on the 84th birthday of its designer, Othmar Ammann, who also designed the George Washington Bridge. The bridge is named after the earliest explorer of the Hudson River.

Under the Verrazano Bridge, the ship channel dredged in the Hudson silt is more than 40 feet deep; this must be dredged to 60 feet to accommodate new enlarged bulk carriers. Left alone, the river and tidal currents would deposit sediments to within about 15 feet of the surface. To allow oceangoing vessels to sail in the Harbor, the U.S. Army Corps of Engineers sucks up the bottom sand and muck, and sometimes contaminated sediments, which they deposit in borrow pits in the New York Bight, or farther out at sea. Man-made islands make good environmental and economic sense; alas, political dinosaurs are not yet ready for them. An artificial island in the New York Bight could accommodate this and other solid wastes. Incidentally, in 2002 I proposed to Mayor Bloomberg the construction of Three R Island, an industrial facility 12 miles out in the New York Bight. Using New technology Three R Island would be a place to recycle city solid waste and convert part of it to electricity. My proposal was rejected. The city now pays dearly to send trainloads of its solid waste to Texas and elsewhere.

We walk toward the north end of Battery Park. Stop to take in the dramatic monument by the sculptor Marisol Escobar mounted in the salty Hudson River, showing a group of merchant seamen adrift on a sinking life

▼ *American Merchant Mariners' Memorial*

raft. A sailor's hand forever reaches up from the dark, cold waters to the desperate men in the small boat. This moving tribute to the men and ships sunk in World War II was installed in 1991.

To the east, glimpse the baroque Custom House south of Bowling Green. This magnificent landmarked beaux-arts-style building, designed by Cass Gilbert and built between 1901 and 1907, incorporates a vast central rotunda with a flat dome on which murals of early New York Harbor scenes were painted by Reginald Marsh. In front of the building, four massive sculptures by Daniel Chester French represent the continents of Asia, America, Europe, and Africa. In 1995, the Custom House became the home of the American Indian Museum, which houses an extraordinary collection of artifacts and information about the first Americans.

Just north of Battery Park we pass an abandoned firehouse on the Fireboat Pier (Pier "A") jutting into the river. Several of New York's fleet of fire-fighting vessels moor here. The city fleet of fireboats has greatly

▼ *A competition of motor pumper engines held by the International Association of Fire Engineers, New York City, September 3, 1913. Pumper engines drew water from the Hudson River.*

Library of Congress/Bain News Service, publisher

diminished since the Container Revolution. Waterfront plans to convert this pier into a restaurant have foundered.

To the east is Bowling Green, a small park that is one reputed site of the "sale" of Manhattan Island by Manahatto Indians to Peter Minuit in 1626. The other reputed and marked site of the $24 transaction is in Inwood Hill Park at the northern end of Manhattan Island. Most Amerindians did not feel any person can really own the land. Perhaps they were right. Bowling Green was a cattle market, a parade ground, and a quasi-public bowling ground before 1732. The iron fence surrounding the park dates to 1771 and is a city landmark. During the American Revolution, an angry mob of colonists toppled an equestrian statue of King George III from its base in the park following the reading of the Declaration of Independence in City Hall Park on July 9, 1776.

On the Hudson shore, directly north of the firehouse pier, is a continuous beautiful waterfront esplanade renamed Robert Wagner Jr. Park in 1996. At the south end, shaped like a bloated fire hydrant, is the Museum of Jewish Heritage (212-968-1800; www.mjhnyc.org). Continue along the charming Battery Park City Esplanade north from Thames Street, past exotic statues and marvelous lush greenery.

A short way to the east of the Hudson Batt-to-Bear path is majestic Trinity Church. When first built, Trinity Church, on Broadway at the foot of Wall Street, overlooked the Hudson River bank. Now, the third church to occupy this site, it stands more than 1,500 feet from the shore. The latest design was executed in 1846 by Richard Upjohn. The church features the Chapel of All Saints and the massive bronze doors by Richard Morris Hunt. The churchyard contains graves of several famous Americans, including Robert Fulton and Alexander Hamilton.

In 1705, England's Queen Anne granted Trinity Church all the land west of Broadway, from Wall Street to Greenwich Village. British troops had expelled the Dutch. I would estimate this sliver of property is worth $50 billion today. Other large Hudson Valley grants were given by English kings and queens to their relatives, followers, and cronies. The American Revolution was fought because most Americans did not subscribe to the "divine right of kings." Yet these royal gifts of land still enrich descendants of royalists (the "east shore family") and in places prevent commoners from walking along American shores.

Continue north along the promenade of Battery Park City, a group of tall apartment buildings built on landfill in the 1960–1980 era. Several small, beautiful parks abut the promenade. North of the promenade is the South Cove, surrounded by a large shore plaza and the striking office buildings of the World Financial Center. Directly westward, the twin towers of the World Trade Center once loomed, surrounded by dramatic landscaping.

On September 11, 2001, fanatics hijacked two jet planes and crashed into the twin towers. The 110-story buildings came down, killing about 3,000 people in the process. A memorial is being constructed on the spot. Several new office towers have already gone up in the area. More are planned under the guidance of the Port Authority of New York and New Jersey.

One World Trade Center is finally going up in 2011. The lead tower will be a 1,776-foot-tall monument. Condé Nast Publications is expected to move about 5,000 employees into 1 million square feet at One World Trade Center sometime in 2014, giving Ground Zero a much-needed corporate anchor with a proven ability to attract other businesses.

On several expeditions in the 1980s, Shorewalkers detoured into the World Trade Center and down a wide escalator to the Port Authority Terminal restrooms. We now prefer the marble toilets of the World Financial Center.

Overlooking South Cove is the capacious glass atrium of the Winter Garden, enclosing stately palm trees somewhat diminished amid the fashionable boutiques and marble staircases. The garden, with its riverside promenade and spacious views of Jersey, overlooks a yacht basin that can accommodate ships 80 to 150 feet long. Gardens and monumental works of art delight the eye. One can slake one's thirst at several nearby restaurants with river views. A recent addition to the area is Poets House, located at 10 River Terrace, overlooking Rockefeller Park (212-431-7920; www.poetshouse.org). Before you leave the area, I also suggest you visit the moving Irish Hunger Memorial at Vesey Street, just north of the World

Financial Center. It is a partially buried structure.

During the roaring 1980s several spectacular buildings sprung up

▲ *Winter Garden, with its palm trees, looking toward the Hudson River*

Christine Yost

along the shore. The Winter Garden, the American Express Tower, and the Shearson-Lehman Tower on Laight Street stand firm, massive, and fortunately good-looking additions to Manhattan's Hudson waterfront.

Across the Hudson River, Jersey City blossomed. Liberty State Park and the Science Museum (built on abandoned railroad yards) dominate the southern shore of Jersey City. Farther north, new waterfront skyscrapers compete aggressively for business with Manhattan's tall office towers.

A gigantic clock, once raised high up on the roof of a Colgate soap factory, now slumps on the ground, its 27-foot minute hand slowly rotating. The factory building it topped has been pulled down to make room for more lucrative condominiums, hotels, and office towers along the Hudson.

North of Jersey City sits Hoboken, 1 square mile of urban delight. Neat rows of two- and three-story brick row houses predominate. Several excellent bars and restaurants are within easy walking distance of the handsome, green, landmarked ferry terminal. Ferry service from the Hoboken terminal to Manhattan and the World Financial Center recommended in the 1990s.

The 42-foot-wide Maxwell House Cup that used to be in front of the shore-side coffee factory is gone and no longer gives off the savory aroma that used to waft across the river. Large office and residential buildings have replaced industrial ship buildings and warehouses that thrived here before 1950.

Hoboken's Stevens Institute, an excellent engineering college (which awarded an honorary doctorate to ex-Hobokenite Frank Sinatra), stands proudly above the Hoboken shore. The artist Alexander Calder was a Stevens graduate.

We continue walking north along Manhattan Island's Hudson shore. Looking east along Murry Street, one can glimpse the top of an imposing Gothic tower, the Woolworth Building. It stands on Broadway overlooking City Hall Park, a sculptured skyscraper conceived by Frank Woolworth, founder of the five-and-ten chain, as a modern office tower. His "cathedral of commerce" was designed in 1913 by Cass Gilbert, who also designed the

Custom House at Bowling Green. This magnificently detailed Gothic-style tower was the tallest in the world until 1930. Look east to see Frank Gehry's 76-story glittering glass tower, now the tallest apartment building in New York City, built in 2011.

Nelson A. Rockefeller Park, a Battery Park City park with a delightful promenade, allows the shorewalker to walk to Chambers Street directly adjacent to the Hudson. The park is a feast to behold and a delight to traverse. This 7-acre stretch of rolling green meadow, built atop landfill, contains perennial gardens, a curving esplanade, and an unusual pavilion. The architect, Demetri Porphyros, describes his column-supported structure as a "dialogue between building and architecture . . ." It is a structure open to the winds, with a belvedere. Dogs and cars—those despoilers of peace—are taboo in this sloping green riverside refuge. The park sports a gazebo and Tom Otterness's family of whimsical brass animals and little humanoids, which delight children (and adults). Lovely plantings, waving grasses, and pretty flowers line the paths.

Until 1992, north of Chambers Street we had to walk on the east side of West Street. We pass Stuyvesant High School, a public school that guides some of America's brightest science students. Catty-corner from Stuyvesant across West Street sits the Borough of Manhattan Community College, a low-rise concrete structure. More than 15,000 diverse students study at this innovative branch of the City University of New York. I taught math there for several years.

From Chambers Street, walk north along the Hudson River Park path through Tribeca, SoHo, and the Village. We see sailing ships, tugs, oil barges, the Circle Line tourist boats, cruise ships, and occasional ocean liners bound for the open sea. Since the Container Revolution of the 1950s, most maritime imports enter New York through the enormous container ports at Newark and Elizabeth, New Jersey, in Newark Bay.

Along the Hudson we see remnants of abandoned piers used for parking lots, warehouses, salt mounds waiting for ice, and ferry terminals. A 10-story rectangular structure, a ventilation tower of the Holland Tunnel

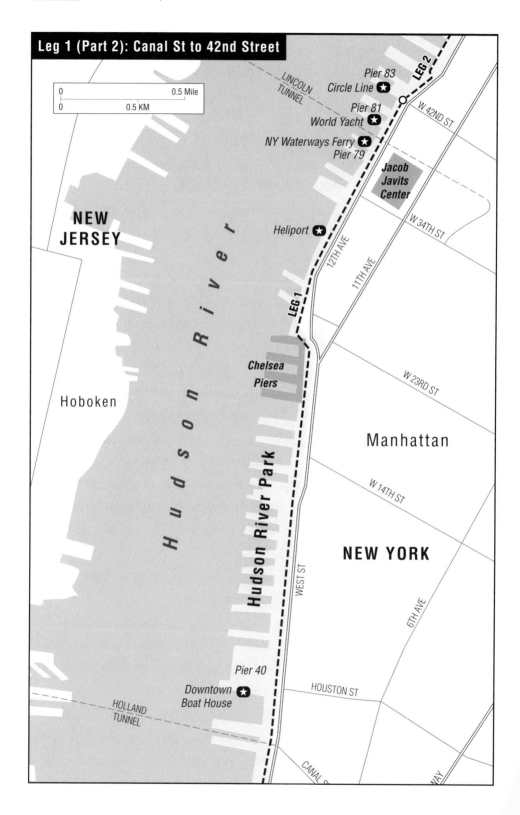

Leg 1 (Part 2): Canal St to 42nd Street

juts up in the river at the end of a Port Authority of New York and New Jersey pier near Canal Street. The Holland Tunnel, named after the engineer who built it, was the first of its kind when constructed in the 1920s and is a landmarked structure.

Looking east we see varied small and medium brick buildings in SoHo and Greenwich Village—some built in Dutch colonial times. Several graceful, cast-iron buildings in Tribeca built in the late 1800s stand out. On Charles Street, the north side of the small, three-story Pathfinder Press building held a striking, huge mural that featured Karl Marx, Malcolm X, Che Guevara, and other radical leaders, but it was erased when the old wall started crumbling. Several new offices and condos have been built along

the Greenwich Village waterfront. Pass New Yorkers and their guests walking, roller skating, biking, and jogging along the river path in all seasons. New York is a walking town. When the weather is pleasant, residents stroll out on the few remaining Hudson piers to sing, read, laze, or hug.

Before 1996, at 12th Street walkers had to leave the river's shore; access was blocked by the New York City Sanitation Department pier, by an MTA bus terminal, and by the Chelsea piers. No shore path was open

Christine Yost

▲ *Special seating along the Hudson River in the Chelsea area.*

for walkers or cyclists. We had to cross West Street to the east side of the roadway and continue north on the sidewalk. Now a walking and biking path can be used. We are now in the Chelsea district.

The Chelsea Piers extend from 14th to 23rd Street. These piers are one of the main accomplishments of the Department of Docks, founded in 1870 to standardize pier size along the bustling, brawling waterfront. Opened in 1910, 30 years after it was first proposed, the Chelsea Piers, New York City's first major passenger ship terminals, were lavishly decorated with allegorical sculptures embedded in concrete and pink granite. Alas, the piers have little industrial or maritime use today. Yachts and party boats tie up in the vicinity of 23rd Street.

In 1995 these large four-story structures were converted into offices, sound studios, a major sports complex, public playgrounds, and a yacht club. The complex can be entered at 18th Street. Toilets and liquids are available. Striking black-and-white photographs of past maritime activity cover the walls. Walk north to 23rd Street. West Street turns into 11th Avenue. Above 23rd Street, one still can get a sweeping view of the great river—marred only by automotive traffic.

Walking on West Street one Sunday morning in 1990, we heard dance music coming from what seemed like an abandoned loft building on West 19th Street. Drawn to the music on the otherwise quiet streets, we entered a cavernous dance club. A handful of dancers, leftovers from Saturday night, moved to the disco beat. Two of my fellow walkers joined the dancers; the rest of us used the washrooms and bought coffee before continuing north.

Erected in 2007 on West Street between 18th and 19th streets, a unique glass and wavy steel office building designed by Frank Gehry glimmers. This is the headquarters of the IAC Corporation (www.iac.com), a conglomerate of some 50 media companies, including Vimeo and the Daily Beast, which recently (2011) swallowed *Newsweek* magazine. The curves in the building facing the river resemble the sails of an enormous windjammer. At night when it is lit up, it stands out spectacularly, especially when seen from nearby

High Line Park (www.thehighline.org), on 10th Avenue.

On the wide Hudson River, kayaks, sailboats, barges pulled by tugs, and oil tankers slowly move about.

North of 23rd Street, large industrial and government buildings line 12th Avenue. From 24th to 26th streets squats a major U.S. postal facility.

To the east between 30th and 34th streets are enormous railroad yards for trains from the Long Island Railroad, AMTRAK, and New Jersey Transit. This area is Manhattan's largest undeveloped land mass. The city has big plans for constructing over the rail yards tall buildings and who knows what. We shall see. Along the river, west of 12th Avenue, helicopters land at the Port Authority 30th Street heliport. Between 30th and 34th streets along the water are New York City automobile tow pounds. Scofflaws and double parkers may find their cars here.

When passing West 34th Street, look to the east to see the majestic Empire State Building, opened in 1929, just in time for the Great

▼ *View of Hudson River, ca. 1875*

Wikimedia Commons/Skinner

▲ *View of and the Empire State Building, taken from the Christopher Street pier*

Depression. It's still a beauty.

From 34th to 39th we tread in the shade of the Javits Convention Center, with its shimmering glass roof. It is among the largest of its kind in North America, with 1.8 million square feet of space on 22 acres of land.

On the shore at West 39th Street, the New York City Department of Transportation has recently built a new ferry terminal, mainly for ferries to New Jersey. Ferries sail to Weehawken across the river in about five minutes. A fleet of 30 buses carries ferry passengers to points in Midtown Manhattan at no cost. Ferry service around Manhattan has expanded greatly since September 2011. One can catch ferries and water taxis to downtown Manhattan, Wall Street (where there is another new ferry terminal), as well as New Jersey. This terminal is an excellent place for shorewalkers to stop for coffee, snacks, water, and toilets.

Christine Yost

North of Hoboken, New Jersey, one can see the Weehawken shore (opposite West 38th Street) where Aaron Burr dueled with the brilliant Alexander Hamilton in 1804 and shot him dead, a great tragedy for the young Republic. Below the cliffs (now a park with a monument) is a broad 100-acre waterfront plot called Slough's Meadow, which up through the 1940s held extensive railroad yards. Cheaper, more flexible, petrol-powered trucks and cars, and new bridges and tunnels, eliminated the need for most trains, ferries, and barges. In the late 1980s, Arthur Imperatore, a dynamic transportation executive, successfully reinstituted ferry service from Weehawken to New York City for a new generation of commuters who prefer to drive to the Weehawken ferry and park, rather than go over the George Washington Bridge or through a tunnel. Imperatore calls this a "civilized commute." Ferries also help keep polluting cars out of the city.

At 40th Street, cross 12th Avenue toward the river, and walk north to the Circle Line at 42nd Street.

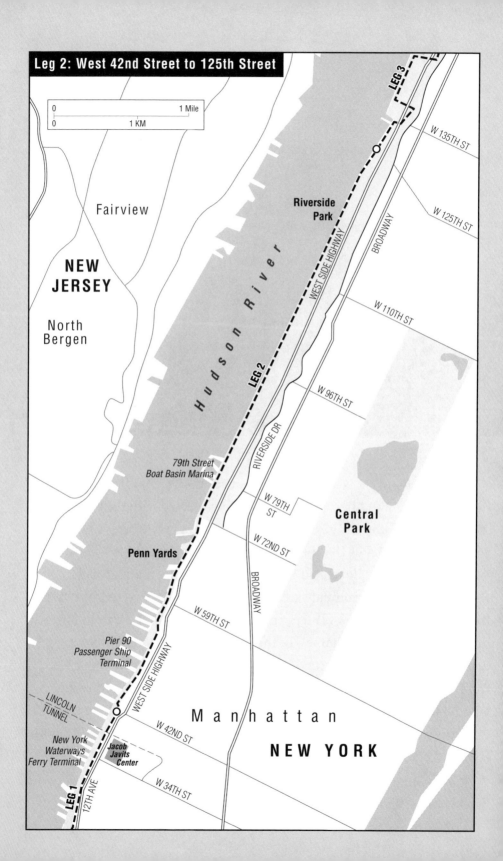

Leg 2: West 42nd Street to 125th Street

LEG 2 | WEST 42ND STREET TO 125TH STREET

ABOUT 4.2 MILES ALONG A CHANGING URBAN AND PARK SHORE

Our life,

much like a river,

Runs always

down to the sea . . .

—Peter Agnos

At the Hudson River and West 42nd Street, one can catch a bus to Times Square (at Seventh Avenue), or to Grand Central Station about 8 avenue blocks (2 miles) east. Better still, one can walk past the theaters, movie houses, outdoor stalls, restaurants, and other delights of dynamic 42nd Street.

The Circle Line (212-563-3200; www.circleline42.com), which docks at West 42nd Street, has a fleet of sight-seeing vessels that completely circle the island of Manhattan. This tour is a unique and wonderful way to savor the watery heritage and delights of New York.

◀ *The* Intrepid, *at the Intrepid Sea, Air & Space Museum, Pier 86, 12th Avenue and 46th Street, New York City*

Wikimedia Commons/Jim from London; *USS Intrepid*, Sea, Air & Space Museum, New York City

45

North of 42nd Street are newly built piers, restaurants, and restrooms. From 42nd to 55th Street, we walk through Hudson River Park along a protected service road abutting the West Side piers. Here cruise ships and ocean liners dock and naval ships visit. The waterfront between 41st and 55th streets is one of the most active tourist hubs along the Hudson shore. At West 46th Street, the Intrepid Sea, Air & Space Museum (212-245-0072; www.intrepidmuseum.org) is in a World War II aircraft carrier now partially sunk in Hudson River mud. This impressive 872-foot hulk was built in 1943. At the time of this writing (2011), a NASA space shuttle prototype is slated to join the other gadgets displayed here, which include a Concorde airliner, a submarine, a navy helicopter carrier, airplanes, and other accoutrements of modern war. Impressive science and space-exploration exhibits are well worth a visit. Occasionally, art, flower, or antiques shows take over the piers. Along this leg one can usually find hot dogs, knishes and assorted New Yorkian nosh delicacies, and toilets.

North of the ocean liner docks are industrial piers 94 (54th Street) to 99 (59th Street). These piers are currently used by a cement maker and by New York's Sanitation Department; the latter uses them as a base from which to ship "solid waste" (garbage) to the Fresh Kills landfill on Staten Island. Fresh Kills was the largest garbage dump in the world, as befits this most active and majestic of American cities. In time, it is slated to become New York City's largest city park. At Pier 98, Con Edison operates a facility mainly as a terminus for gas and oil, which is pumped from tankers to

▼ *The coastline of legs 1, 2, and 3, with a view of the Jersey shore*

a stately, block-long white stone generator building. It is topped by one remaining 500-foot-high smokestack. In the 20th century, when the plant burned coal from its opening through the 1940s, four smokestacks belched black smoke. Now Con Edison's major fuels are gas (50 percent) and nuclear (35 percent), and New York City's air is cleaner.

From 59th to 72nd Street, shorewalkers' preferred walking route was a dirt road through a "secret garden" in the abandoned Penn Railroad Yards. They were open to walkers and bikers for many years when the defunct railroads owned the property. On a spring morning in 1979 while bicycling to work through the Penn Yards, I came upon a Barnum and Bailey Circus train parked along the river. Animals, clowns, and lion tamers walked about. Circus performers munched on sandwiches, hung out laundry to dry, walked their dogs . . . an unexpected, charming sight. My neighbors and other walkers used the Penn Yards for many years as a public thoroughfare that much quieter, more scenic, and safer than West End Avenue (the extension of 11th Avenue) to the west. The stately Miller Highway viaduct, refurbished in

The Secret Garden

By CY A ADLER

In "The Selfish Giant," Oscar Wilde tells of a giant who built a high wall to keep children out of his garden. While the giant was on vacation in Cornwall visiting a friendly ogre, neighborhood children broke into his garden to play.

"It was a large, lovely garden with soft green grass. Here and there over the grass stood beautiful flowers like stars. The birds sat in the trees and sang so sweetly that the children used to stop their games in order to listen.

"How happy we are," they cried to each other.

After a seven-year visit with his friend, the Cornish ogre, the giant returned. When he arrived he saw the children playing in the garden.

"What are you doing there?" he cried in a very gruff voice, and the children ran away.

"My own garden is my own garden," said the giant.

"Anyone can understand that, and I will allow nobody to play in it but myself." So he built a high wall all around it and put up a notice board:

Trespassers Will Be Prosecuted

He was a very selfish giant.

What, you may ask, happened next in Oscar Wilde's story?

Well, as a consequence of the giant's high wall, sunshine and happiness deserted the garden. Nothing would grow there. This saddened the giant.

But the story has a happy ending. I will not destroy your pleasure of reading for yourself how it turned out.

Along the Hudson River in Manhattan is a large, beautiful, open space where one finds waving reeds, bright morning glories, grasses, varied wild flowers, including the majestic Queen Anne's lace.

This green space, called the Penn Yards, runs from 59th to 72d Streets, from the Hudson River to 11th Avenue. It used to be a busy railroad yard . . . no trains stop there now.

Before 1981 the Penn Yards area was used by New Yorkers as a quiet place to walk or to bicycle or just to sit and watch the river. I bicycled to work for three years along the wide dirt road that runs parallel to the Hudson River through The Penn Yards.

This pleasant road is the natural northern extension of 12th Avenue and on old city maps was so designated. By traversing north, 12th Avenue walkers and bicyclists avoided noisy and hazardous traffic along 11th and West End Avenues.

Using North 12th Avenue, a cyclist can go all the way from Uptown Manhattan — Washington Heights, Harlem or the Upper West Side — to 42d Street without encountering a single stop-light or a car.

North 12th Avenue is a vital and natural segment of the Hudson River Shore Trail, a 330-mile greenway, which will go from the mouth of the river at the Battery to the river's source somewhere high in the Adirondacks.

Before 1980 I led groups of hikers through the yards along North 12th Avenue on our way to the Little Red Lighthouse.

Near the lighthouse shorewalkers pay respects to the white sock, which has hiked along the shore of Lake Tear-of-the-Clouds on Mount Marcy.

The sock is buried in a shoe box (with the gerbil Gerb) in the shade of the George Washington Bridge.

In 1981 the Penn Yards property was sold by the railroad to a would-be developer who erected a high, barbed-wire fence to keep New Yorkers out. The developer displayed shiny brochures of his grandiose plans, then sold the property to the Trump Organization in 1985.

Opening up North 12th Avenue to pedestrians and cyclists will save lives and make New York City a more agreeable place in which to live and work.

Congested Manhattan needs open breathing space; it does not want for high-rise buildings below 125th Street, and lives can be saved if bikers were to travel from 59th to 72d Streets along North 12th Avenue rather than detour along avenues thick with traffic.

In densely populated cities, open space is a necessity of inestimable value.

For more than 10 years, New Yorkers have been deprived of their historic right of innocent passage through Penn Yards park — for a park is what in essence it is.

To keep this large, airy Manhattan Park locked up and useless for years — perhaps for decades — is a crime against good civic sense.

The giant in Oscar Wilde's story knocked down the fence, lived contentedly with his neighbors and died happy.

1993 and 1994 at a public cost of some $90 million, floats 70 feet above the Penn Yards, leaving the ground below relatively quiet and free from air pollution. Certain well-meaning (?) citizens tried to tear down the Miller viaduct and replace it with a trench similar to the Cross-Bronx Expressway at a cost estimated to be $200 million. This project did not go through, which saddened the landlords who own apartment buildings overlooking the Miller Highway. Former mayor Giuliani attempted to rename the Miller Highway the Joe DiMaggio Highway. I prefer the name Miller Highway, which commemorates a Manhattan borough president who helped New York grow and prosper.

In 1985 the Penn Yards were closed to the public by "developers," most notably builder Donald Trump. In 1995 Trump sold a majority interest in the site to a group of Hong Kong investors/speculators. Walkers had to detour east along 59th Street to West End Avenue, go north to 72nd, and then east back to Riverside Park. We were told we could not go through the property because it was unsafe. However, landowners who give public easements are protected from negligence suits in New York State.

In May 1992, due to the requests of Shorewalkers, its friends, and its advisors, the Great Saunter of 1992 around Manhattan Island was allowed to walk through the Penn Yards for the first time in more than ten years.

▼ *Flying kites from the pier at 69th Street.*

Christine Yost

About 50 shorewalkers passed under the soaring viaduct on the firm dirt roadbed along the Hudson and then through a hole in the fence into Riverside Park.

▼ *At the entrance to Riverside Park*

Wikimedia Commons/Paranormal Skeptic

From 59th to 72nd streets, walkers can now amble through Riverside Park South. This beautiful new park sports undulating waterfront trails separated from a bike lane under the main highway. You will find a restaurant near 70th Street, a long pier, and toilets.

Riverside Park, a flawed emerald necklace gracing the west flank of Manhattan, was built on railroad rights-of-way, rocky outcrops, and landfill by public pressure, accident, and Robert Moses. Frederick Law Olmsted, F. Stewart Williamson, and other architects also worked toward the creation of this waterside park with magnificent vistas. They designed the narrow sloping greenway to run along Manhattan's rocky west shore's spine, harmoniously setting off the glades, playing fields, and promenades below. Robert Moses expanded the park considerably when he built the West Side Highway in the 1930s.

The major defect of Riverside Park is the six-lane, ground-level roadway that runs through the heart of the park, carrying thousands of noisy cars. When Robert Moses built the highway, he covered over the New York Central rail line, which runs parallel to and east of the highway. Riverside Drive residents were delighted when the then-active smelly, smoky cattle cars and noisy freight trains were out of sight and sound, buried in a 75-foot-wide tunnel from 123rd Street to 72nd Street. Alas, he did not cover the six-lane automotive roadway and extend Riverside Park to the river.

For several years Shorewalkers and other citizens have helped clean up the park and pick up debris along the Hudson River Shore Trail west of the roadway. Most of the trash comes from drivers who dispose of plastics, beer cans, bottles, and other trash via their car windows. When the west flank path is sufficiently widened to about 3 feet—and the citizens of New York reclaim the use of Penn Yards' delightful shore road—bikers and walkers will have a riverside path clear of cars from 42nd Street to 130th Street.

Incidentally, it is worth noting that most Manhattan residents—some 70 percent of households—do not own cars because of excellent mass transit and the compactness of the city. Owning relatively few cars, and being mostly apartment dwellers, New Yorkers are among the most energy-efficient citizens in the country. (See "Cars are Like Dogs in the City.")

Christine Yost

◀ *Time for a bite and beverage at the 79th Street boat basin, with the Hudson River in view.*

After entering Riverside Park at 72nd, veer west to the asphalt river promenade. At 79th Street is a large marina, the only one along this coast operated by the New York City Parks Department. This waterlogged residential community of about 70 vessels is not a good stopover for passing vessels. Most of the ships are grounded with their keels in the mud since the siltation rate is great. At low tide only about a foot of water stands in most of the marina. Gasoline is no longer available at the 79th Street marina, and most of

Cars Are Like Dogs in the City
By Cyrus A Adler

In large cities, cars should be treated like dogs. Dogs and cars diminish the pleasures of living and working in cities. Like dogs, but more so, cars are a menace to municipal life, an impediment to the freedom of walkers, a destroyer of civic pleasures. Cars have grown into a plague that, if allowed to continue unabated, will destroy the city.

The automobile is by far the major cause of air pollution in most of our cities and a major cause of water pollution due to sewer runoff of waste oil. With trucks and buses, the car is the prime creator of city street noise.

Like dog owners, car owners should be forced to clean up after their pets--to pay for cleaning the air and water they foul, fixing the streets they destroy and lowering the noise they generate. Cynics said New York City politicians did not have the guts to pass a law requiring dog owners to clean up after their pets; if a law was passed, dog owners would ignore it. It took much persuasion and years of lobbying to get city officials to curb dog owners.

Cars can also be curbed--indeed, must be if our cities are to be healthy and pleasant places in which to live and work. Raising tolls on bridges and speedways, limiting parking space and towing away offenders are good beginnings but will not suffice to keep the car- crazed from driving about the city in their big buggies.

The best way to accommodate automotive traffic in cities is to bury it in tunnels. Burying traffic gives the streets back to the people, to us bipeds and bicyclists. Cars--most of which are not essential--should be forced to travel in tun-

nels beneath cities alongside trucks and buses--leaving the surface roads for pedestrians, bikers and small cars designed specifically for cities.

Battery Park in Manhattan is an example. The park is a delight for walkers, loungers and lovers. Yet beneath the park runs a major truck and car route. Citizens have here reclaimed the surface of their city and can taste the pleasures of open space and quiet in a greensward by the water.

Frederick Law Olmsted made Central Park a saunterer's delight by submerging most of the crosstown traffic through the park. Unfortunately, he did not go far enough. He should also have submerged the north-south roads and covered them over. Even the visionary Olmsted could not foresee the car plague.

Many of our streets can be converted into car-free zones and public, pedestrian malls. Our city is made liveable by open spaces such as Rockefeller Center, Nassau Street, the South Street Seaport area, Washington Square, Columbia University's campus and waterfront cul-de-sacs, former streets that are now car-free zones.

In well-run, compact cities with a variety of buses, trains, and taxis, and with relatively concentrated business and pleasure districts, cars are rarely needed. Munich, Copenhagen, Beijing and other cities have banned dogs or cars from their central districts. If we also would prefer cities where we can saunter with our friends along quiet promenades, breathing fresh air and talking in normal tones, then we must act together to limit the kinds and the movement of cars. ☐

Sierra Atlantic

the vessels have had their engines removed to reduce the fire hazard and insurance costs. Many of the boat owners are vocal and talented; they are a varied group of New Yorkers dedicated to this unique, relatively low-rent, houseboat-colony way of urban life.

Incidentally, if left to nature, the entire lower Hudson estuary would naturally silt up to about 16 feet. To allow deep-water vessels to sail 150 miles north to Albany, the main Hudson channel must be excavated to about 40 feet. Dredging the channels is (or should be) done continuously by the U.S. Army Corps of Engineers.

For several years, active discussions have ensued as to what is the best way to dispose of these dredge spoils, some of which are contaminated. Dump them at sea, drop them in borrow pits, or build a containment

Christine Yost

▲ *View of a red-tailed hawk's nest through a photographer's viewfinder, around 82nd Street in Riverside Park*

Christine Yost

▲ *A winter view of the Batt to Bear path along the Hudson River, Manhattan*

island for them? Man-made islands have been built in Japan and Hong Kong. Even New York City can boast several such islands, including most of Ellis and Governors and Rikers. These were built up mostly with debris, trash, sand, and dredged silt. In the long run, containment islands make good environmental and economic sense. New York is fortunate in having a shallow coastal plain close to its shore on which large industrial islands can be constructed. We propose construction of Three R Island for industrial purposes in the New York Bight.

Boat owners who use the 79th Street marina can park their cars in an underground garage opposite the marina, underneath the 79th Street grade elimination structure. This three-layer marvel of engineering and road design was built in the 1934–1937 era, during the Great Depression.

At 79th Street, Moses's engineers built a circular marble fountain over the Penn Central railroad tracks surrounded by a vaguely Moorish cloister.

Until the 1990s, some of New York's homeless found shelter under this beautiful rotunda, in this richest of all cities in this most powerful of all countries. In summer, concerts and plays are performed under the vaulted structure looking out over the river. Hosted by men in sleek tuxedos and women in black

▼ *Grant's Tomb and Riverside Church in Riverside Park*

Wikimedia Commons/Roger Rowlett

gowns, benefits are held to raise money for good causes. A bar/restaurant operates here in warm weather.

In the 2000–2010 decade, the narrow rutted path that formerly had to be traversed by walkers at this point was bypassed by a solid causeway jutting over the Hudson. To the east, Mount Tom, a rocky hump of black gneiss, rises near Riverside Drive at 83rd Street. Mount Tom was a favored spot for Edgar Allan Poe to view the Jersey shore when he summered near here on West 84th Street in the 1840s. Kids romp on it.

At 86th Street we may glimpse the Clarendon apartments built on Riverside Drive in 1907. William Randolph Hearst lived in the upper five floors with his animals, family, and motley collection of art objects and junk. At 89th Street stand the tall white marble pillars of the Soldiers' and Sailors' Monument, dedicated to the dead of the Civil War and all subsequent American wars. New York's then governor, Theodore Roosevelt, laid the cornerstone in 1899, some 34 years after the edifice was proposed. It was completed in 1912. On Memorial Day, veterans of various wars gather here to beat drums, mourn, and make speeches. Toilets and bathrooms can be found in the West 80s or 90s. We walk past clay tennis courts, anglers, runners, bikers, lovers, and picnickers. At 90th Street we must take the so-called Cherry Walk in Riverside Park.

▼ *Grant's Tomb, Morningside Heights, New York City*

Wikimedia Commons/Nightscream

▼ *A fleet of U.S. Navy battleships sail past Grant's Tomb in Manhattan during World War I.*

Wikimedia Commons/Brown Brothers

Note the narrow dirt "Desire Path" made by walkers and runners to avoid bikers.

To the west, stone riprap leads down to the Hudson; the Henry Hudson Highway runs to the east. This greenway boasts beautiful locust, ailanthus, and cherry trees, which look pretty year-round but are a special delight during their brief season of bloom in May when the Great Saunter passes by. A path winds among the trees, which grow more varied—here a honey locust, there an oak or hawthorn. The hawthorn, a hardy city tree, grows on the Broadway mall and beside housing projects where few other trees can survive.

Approaching Harlem, the cherry walk narrows as the highway squeezes riverward. At 120th Street, Riverside Church's tall white tower, with its caroling bells, stands to the east. The tower observation room, open to the public, affords spectacular views of the river

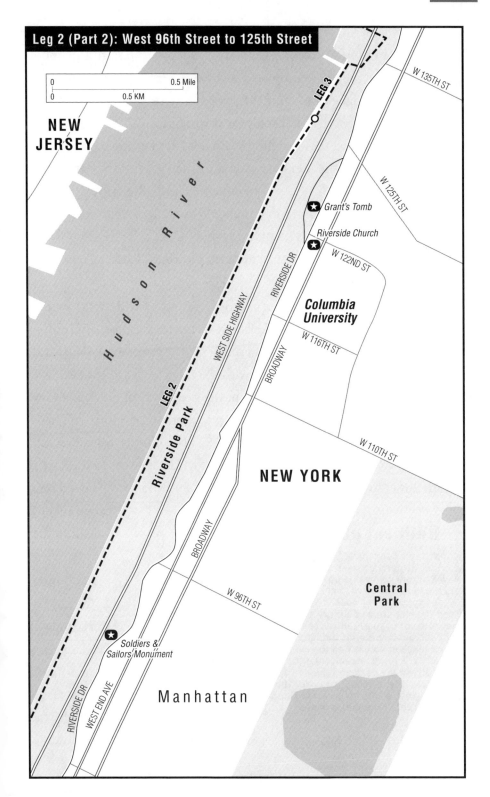

Leg 2 (Part 2): West 96th Street to 125th Street

0   0.5 Mile
0   0.5 KM

NEW JERSEY

Hudson River

LEG 3

W 135TH ST

★ Grant's Tomb
Riverside Church
★

W 125TH ST

RIVERSIDE DR

W 122ND ST

WEST SIDE HIGHWAY

Columbia University

W 116TH ST

BROADWAY

LEG 2

Riverside Park

W 110TH ST

NEW YORK

BROADWAY

Central Park

W 96TH ST

★ Soldiers & Sailors Monument

RIVERSIDE DR

WEST END AVE

Manhattan

and the Jersey shore. Below it sits Grant's Tomb. Great trees line the upper promenade leading to the tomb. Grant and his wife sleep in this cylinder atop a square base that was completed in 1897. Its environs are enlivened by brightly tiled benches and animal forms put there by neighborhood people under the supervision of sculptor Pedro Silva. I think the sculptures charming; others detest them, calling them a form of graffiti. A few hundred yards west of the concrete walk is a small gravestone surrounded by an old iron fence. Dedicated to "an amiable child," the gravestone was placed here in Colonial times, more than 200 years ago. Major institutions to the east in Harlem Heights include Teachers College, Columbia University; the Union and Jewish seminaries; Barnard College; and the Manhattan School of Music.

At 125th Street we enter Harlem and descend into a wide, flat, riverside plaza running for several city blocks between the now-closed Hudson View Diner and the New York City garbage transfer station at 135th Street. The diner, under the roadway with the train tracks above, was a favorite spot for walkers, truck drivers of the nearby meat market, and taxi and bus drivers. It served ample, inexpensive, somewhat Southern fare. Unfortunately, the IRS closed it down in 1992. The hungry hiker can raid the large Fairway, which opened in 1996, or detour 2 blocks to the east on 125th Street to McDonald's or Burger King on Broadway. Several bar-restaurants have opened in the vicinity.

Along the 125th–128th Street Hudson plaza, one can sit on the squares of planters. On weekends when the weather is

Eminent plan to trump Donald

Manhattan: Your June 24 editorial on the imaginary Hudson shore strip park between 59th and 72nd Sts. should enrage all New Yorkers who value open space. Land speculators who control the old Penn Yards have kept New Yorkers out for too long.

As I explain in my book, "Walking the Hudson, Batt to Bear," Penn Central allowed bikers and walkers through the site. But they sold out to an Argentine speculator in the 1980s who fenced it off and public officials did nothing. Then Donald Trump came in and blocked access and the city did nothing. Now the land is owned by Hong Kong speculators who still block passage between Riverside Park and the new Hudson River Park.

It's time city officials take over this land by eminent domain and integrate it into an emerald chain along the Hudson for all New Yorkers. Open the park now. *Cy Adler*

Tuesday, July 7, 1998 • DAILY NEWS

good, locals wash their cars, people fish from the dock, and other citizens gaze at the water and walk about. Spanish, Chinese, Korean, Haitian, and various dialects of English can be heard along this shore. Until about 1950, a long, two-level recreational pier and dock served passengers taking the Hudson River Day steamers to Albany or the ferry to New Jersey.

Persons wishing to join or leave the walk can do so at 125th Street. The #1 Broadway Local train stops on Broadway close to the shore. The Broadway bus can take you south; a crosstown 125th Street bus goes to the east and to an express Metro-North train station.

> JUNE 29-JULY 6, 1998
>
> ### THE NEW YORK OBSERVER
>
> **DUMP THE DITCH**
>
> To the Editor:
> Your article on the Miller Highway ["Tricky Donald Trump Beats Jerry Nadler in Game of Politics," June 8] omitted pertinent points about this historic arterial road.
> Replacing this arterial with a ditch ("submerged highway") along which cars would take a circuitous path would increase vehicular path-length, air pollution at ground level, automotive noise at ground level and decrease open space available to the public. I estimate about 300,000 square feet of land would be lost.
> Many pleasant memories come to mind of times I have walked and biked the Hudson path along the Miller Highway. I have led groups of walkers along the path from West 59th to 72nd streets and encountered no air pollution, almost no noise, no danger. Wildflowers and grasses bloomed along the side of the road. One can think of the existing aerial structure as a colonnade of stately trees which give shade and shelter and yet allows human passage. Then consider the $300 million alternative: a noisy, smelly ditch.
> CY A. ADLER
> *Manhattan*

It is always wise to keep your eyes peeled for possible hazards when walking in unfamiliar neighborhoods. We recommend walking this beautiful area during daylight with companions.

In 2009 New York City completed construction of West Harlem Pier Park, with sparkling piers for fishing and lounging, and hopefully for ferries. The waterfront area has improved considerably since 1985—from a decrepit meat market to a lively space with a big Fairway market, several upscale restaurants, and a pretty park.

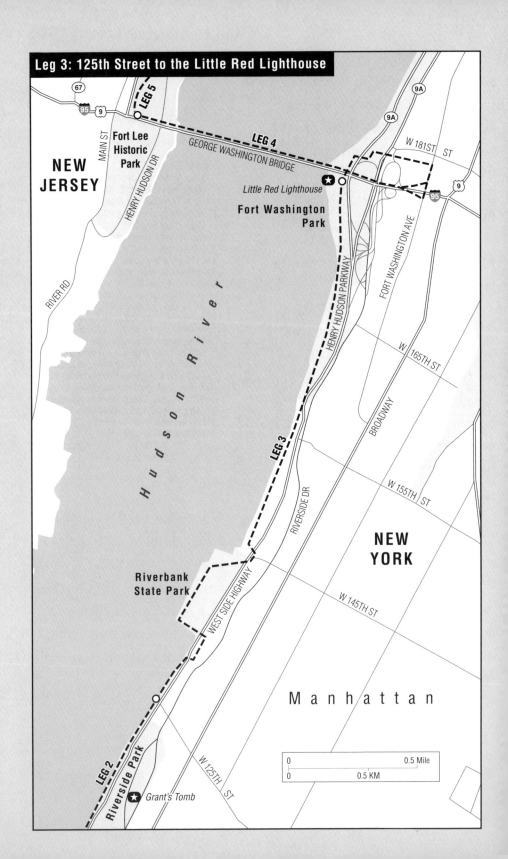

Leg 3: 125th Street to the Little Red Lighthouse

67

95 9

LEG 5

MAIN ST

HENRY HUDSON DR

Fort Lee Historic Park

NEW JERSEY

GEORGE WASHINGTON BRIDGE

LEG 4

9A

9A

W 181ST ST

9

95

Little Red Lighthouse

Fort Washington Park

FORT WASHINGTON AVE

RIVER RD

H u d s o n   R i v e r

HENRY HUDSON PARKWAY

W 165TH ST

BROADWAY

LEG 3

RIVERSIDE DR

W 155TH ST

NEW YORK

Riverbank State Park

WEST SIDE HIGHWAY

W 145TH ST

M a n h a t t a n

0		0.5 Mile
0	0.5 KM	

LEG 2

Riverside Park

W 125TH ST

Grant's Tomb

LEG 3 | 125TH STREET TO THE LITTLE RED LIGHTHOUSE

ABOUT 3 MILES, MOSTLY THROUGH PARKS

Come walk with us along the still-green banks.

—Cy A Adler

◀ *An alternate ground route along the Manhattan Greenway around Riverbank State Park should save about 10 minutes for walkers in a hurry, but then one will miss the magnificent views, food, and toilets of Riverbank State Park.*

From the new piers opened in May 2009 along the 125th Street waterfront, we scan the Palisades of Jersey. If it is raining, we usually walk under the Riverside Drive viaduct and railroad trestle, an awesome massive steel and stone elevated structure. At 135th Street, we usually go under the viaduct into a sliver of Riverside Park, and then up a majestic but crumbling and seedy granite stairway to Riverside Drive.

On several expeditions during the 1980s we walked along the level, then-unused railroad tracks, thus avoiding the climb to Riverside Drive. From 1982 to 1990 no trains used the tracks. For 60 years, until 1982, this was a major freight line bringing meat, livestock, and freight of various kinds to New York. In the 1970s traffic dwindled to a few loads of large paper rolls for the *New York Times* and other large users. A community garden grows on the slope between Riverside Drive and the tracks.

In 1990 the rail track along the river was refurbished. The Spuyten Duyvil turn bridge over the Harlem River is again functioning, and fast passenger trains run from Albany directly to Penn Station—what is left of it. Therefore, it is no longer wise to walk along the railroad track.

Around 2003, in a section of the Manhattan Waterfront Greenway, a bike path was paved adjacent to the sewage plant. This can be walked, but we prefer the following: Having climbed the giant, gray, stone staircase, topped by a huge stone urn, we gain the wide promenade along Riverside Drive, a winding majestic road that affords a bird's-eye view of the North River Pollution Control Plant. It may be called something more fetching, such as "water purification" or "environmental improvement plant," but it is the terminus for most West Side sewers from Greenwich Village to the northern tip of Manhattan. This impressive 28-acre concrete structure was built in the early 1970s, mostly with federal funds. Shorewalkers were given a tour of the facility in 1989. Enormous efforts have gone into keeping the

▼ *Looking east from Rappers Row in Gutenberg across the Hudson River at Riverbank State Park and the sewage plant*

odors down. Alas, it is the nature of feces and urine to stink. But odors were barely noticeable on our recent passages along Riverside Drive.

In 1993, New York State built a large public park on top of the sewer plant, between 137th and 145th streets, called Riverbank State Park (212-694-3600; www.nysparks.state.ny.us). It is a remarkable recreational facility funded through city, state, and federal programs, reflecting strong public commitment to enriching the quality of life in New York City.

At 137th and 145th streets, graceful and substantial pedestrian bridges over the highway and rail tracks connect the rocky heights of Riverside Drive to the park. The park's pools, tracks, and playing fields are well worth visiting. Breathtaking vistas, clean toilets, water, and snacks are available most of the year. We usually enter the park over the south bridge at 137th Street from Riverside Drive, walk through it, enjoy its views and facilities, and then exit at the north end of 145th Street via a winding steel staircase to shore level 50 feet below. Continue north through green playing fields of Riverside Park and then a row of sycamore trees. This area is very active in summertime, with Spanish the predominant spoken language you'll hear.

Riverside Drive was a symbol of new wealth from the 1890s to the 1920s, when it was popular with rich businessmen. The drive's ornate, curlicued

facades showed off the millions of their moneyed inhabitants. The "old money" living off their inheritances from George III, and the profits from rum, slavery, and other early American enterprises, preferred Park and Fifth avenues and Sutton Place on the east side of Manhattan. In my opinion, Riverside Drive's location, fine parks, and clean air surpass those of any other avenue in Manhattan. The air on the west side of Manhattan

Wikimedia Commons/Jim Henderson

is, on average, less polluted
than the air on the east side,
due to the westerly winds
that waft air pollution to Park
Avenue and Sutton Place.

Library of Congress/Bain News Service, publisher

Cross the solid footbridge
over the rail tracks into the
northern part of Riverside
Park, a flat and open stretch
of green. Here are handball
and basketball courts, large
parking lots, picnic tables

▲ *Ice in the Hudson at 148th Street,*
  ca. 1910–1915

between the West Side Highway and the river, as well as views of the
George Washington Bridge, the wide river, and the Jersey Palisades.

Six geese in tight V formation flew swiftly north, low over the water,
as we walked this way in mid-June of 1990. Two glistening mallards sat,
statuesque and still, on an upturned car chassis half sunk in the near-shore
muck. A dozen or more large full-leafed mulberry trees grew at the river's
edge. Two trees grow right up through the riprap consisting here of a slope
of large boulders, concrete blocks, and stones placed along the river shore
to slow its inevitable erosion.

▼ *Henry Hudson Parkway and the George Washington Bridge*

Here along the river's edge it is relatively free of car noise since the Henry Hudson Parkway is elevated as it slowly climbs to Washington Heights and the entrance to the George Washington Bridge. On occasion, I have walked north above the park along Riverside Drive. A majestic walk, despite the cars whizzing by. Trinity Cemetery, the largest in Manhattan, runs from 153rd to 155th Street, sloping up to Amsterdam Avenue. Some of New York's most magnificent trees grow there. The artist Audubon is buried there. Calvert Vaux, a partner of F. L. Olmsted in the creation of Central Park, designed the cemetery gatehouse in the 1880s.

Directly north of quiet Trinity Cemetery is a collection of classical stone buildings housing the Hispanic Museum, with a fabulous collection of Goyas, and Spanish-speaking Boricua College.

Continue north along the Great Saunter footpath (also the Manhattan Greenway) for a quarter of a mile, walking close to the Hudson shore. On a Sunday in May three men were fishing and crabbing in the shade of a locust tree that sprouted from large rough riprap at the water's edge. Cormorants competed for the fishermen's catch. This flock of black, long-necked diving birds has flourished as the Hudson's water has become cleaner since the 1980s. We pass basketball courts under the highway viaduct only a dozen yards from the quiet river's edge as we enter Fort Washington Park.

Wikimedia Commons/Roger Rowlett

Fort Washington Park extends along the Hudson River from 158th Street to Dyckman Street. Below Washington Heights we encounter playing fields that we must walk through or around. If you take the weedy path west of the extensive playing fields and picnic areas along the water's edge, at one badly eroded

section you must hang onto the chain-link fence or face the possibility of falling into the river. It is safer to walk through the playing fields.

Fort Washington Park, green and beautiful, is less used than Riverside Park because it is more isolated and difficult to reach. Pedestrians must negotiate winding paths over and under a maze of highways, cloverleafs, and a railroad line to reach the park.

At West 170th we pass the playing fields and come out on a spacious open area of fields and trees within clear sight of the Little Red Lighthouse, with the silver George Washington Bridge looming above it and the majestic Palisades beyond.

The steel tubular lighthouse we see was built in 1880. It originally stood guard at Sandy Hook, New Jersey. In 1921, the U.S. Coast Guard moved it to Jeffrey's Hook to prevent the extensive Hudson River shipping traffic from piling up on the rocks near the rocky coast. The George

◀ *(Top to bottom)*

Fort Washington Park, as seen from the great George Washington Bridge in 2011

Two distant views of the Little Red Lighthouse from the George Washington Bridge

The Little Red Lighthouse at Jeffrey's Hook, Manhattan

Wikimedia Commons/Equipe C'est N'est Pas Une Pipe

Washington Bridge opening in 1937 made the little lighthouse obsolete. To add further insult, salt combined with pigeon droppings from the bridge above rusted and eroded the cast-iron lighthouse. Hard-nosed Coast Guard auditors decided to demolish it. But in 1942, Hildegarde Hoyt Smith wrote a children's book, *The Little Red Lighthouse and the Great Gray Bridge*, that generated a public outcry against demolition. This persuaded New York City parks commissioner Robert Moses to transfer the lighthouse to city ownership in 1951. Thus a rusting cylinder was added to the National Register of Historic Places in 1979 and landmarked in 1991.

One can still climb the narrow circular staircase to the glass-enclosed light room for a spectacular river view 40 feet above the rocks. However, the building is usually locked by the NYC Parks Department to prevent vandalism. It is opened for tours and special occasions.

U.S. Hydrographic Chart 12341 shows clearly how the Hudson River narrows in the vicinity of Jeffrey's Point, now part of Fort Washington Park. The river's depth reaches more than 70 feet not far from the Little Red Lighthouse, marked "ABAND. L.H." on sailing charts. Here the great river estuary narrows to 1,100 yards. As predicted by mathematician Bernoulli, this constriction forces the tidal stream to flow swifter here than anywhere else along the Manhattan shore.

Water fountains in the park under the bridge work during warm-weather months. Sit on benches or on the rocks near the lighthouse to breathe in the salt air and take in the sight of the timeless Palisades beneath the graceful bridge with its lacelike towers. Most of the car drivers crawl along, oblivious of the beauty around them. Architect and designer Le Corbusier called the George Washington Bridge "the most beautiful bridge in the world. Made of cables and steel beams, it gleams in the sky like an up-turned arch. It is blessed . . ."

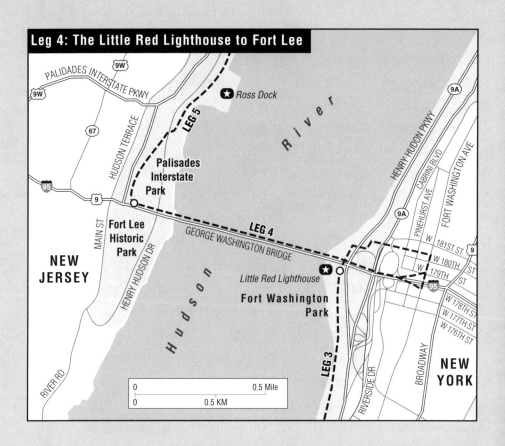

Leg 4: The Little Red Lighthouse to Fort Lee

PALIDADES INTERSTATE PKWY

9W

9W

67

95

9

HUDSON TERRACE

LEG 5

★ Ross Dock

River

Palisades
Interstate
Park

MAIN ST

Fort Lee
Historic
Park

HENRY HUDSON DR

NEW
JERSEY

Hudson

GEORGE WASHINGTON BRIDGE

LEG 4

Little Red Lighthouse

Fort Washington
Park

LEG 3

RIVER RD

RIVERSIDE DR

BROADWAY

9A

HENRY HUDON PKWY

CABRINI BLVD

PINEHURST AVE

FORT WASHINGTON AVE

9A

W 181ST ST

W 180TH
ST

W 179TH
ST

9

95

W 178TH ST

W 177TH ST

W 176TH ST

NEW
YORK

0   0.5 Mile

0   0.5 KM

LEG 4

THE LITTLE RED LIGHTHOUSE TO FORT LEE

TWO MILES UP AND OVER THE GEORGE WASHINGTON BRIDGE

Our misty world

Is indeed a world of dew;

And yet . . .

—*K. Issa*

Exiting Fort Washington Park from the Little Red Lighthouse on foot is not simple because of the adjacent spaghetti-like maze of highways under the George Washington Bridge near 179th Street. At least eight roads, two railroad tracks, dirt paths, and cloverleaf lobes twist and undulate between the park and the upper levels of Washington Heights. Incidentally, General Washington had built a string of forts upon the bluffs, but he abandoned them to the British during the War for Independence. Almost no trace of them remains except for street place-names and a plaque in Bennett Park.

The car-studded ribbons of concrete below the bridge are not friendly to pedestrians. To cross and exit from the maze of roads and rails below the bridge at the Little Red Lighthouse on the north, one must climb the asphalt path under the bridge toward 181st Street. The terrain outcrop is solid rock: basal magma and schist that underlie New York Island. Walk east over the footbridge train trestle and through a rock tunnel running under Riverside Drive. Switchback north to a pedestrian bridge over Riverside Drive, thus exiting Fort Washington Park. Walk east to, and then south along, Fort Washington Avenue to 179th Street. In the Port Authority bus terminals one can find coffee and toilets. Two concrete walkways exit: one to the north and one to the south of the bridge's upper roadway. Turn west on 179th Street and walk a few hundred feet to Cabrini Boulevard, where you will see a narrow metal staircase that leads to the north and the walkway on the bridge. To take the southern walkway, turn west on 178th Street instead of 179th, and ascend the cloverleaf ramp to the upper deck of the bridge.

Crossing the George Washington Bridge on the shared bicycle footpaths is an exhilarating experience not to be missed by any lover of nature or of cities. The spectacular walk—about 1.5 miles—is worth the

▼ *Sunset and clouds over the George Washington Bridge*

200-plus-foot climbs at either end.

Most splendid (in my opinion) of all Manhattan crossings, the George Washington Bridge drapes silvery filigree across the wide, salty estuary between the sovereign states of New York and New Jersey. The George Washington Bridge celebrated its 80th anniversary in 2011. From a distance, it looks like a silver necklace held up by two strong yet supple decorated pillars. From close up, the steel web, supported by harplike cables, dominates the hills of upper Manhattan, the cliff dwellings on either shore, and the Palisades 300 feet high above the Hudson at Fort Lee.

Two tall, open-lattice steel towers support the main catenary suspension cables; the graceful vertical harp stays holding the roadbeds, the concrete roadway, and the two walking paths on either side of the upper road all combine in a simple yet wonderfully engineered system of supports and tensions. Each component works with the others to allow thousands of cars, trucks, buses, and humans to cross the wide Hudson estuary daily. Car drivers rarely get to savor the ineffable majesty of the surroundings.

Only the walker can fully appreciate the majesty of the bridge and its panoramic expanse.

The bridge's overall length is 4,760 feet between anchorages; its deck is 115 feet wide. It took four years to build. In 1962 it was double-decked to become the world's first 16-lane suspension bridge with a roadway peaking at 212 feet above mean high water. The decks are held up by four mighty cables, each 3 feet in diameter, composed of 26,474 parallel wires. From the tower top to the trough of the catenary, in the form of a hanging chain, is 316 feet. Stop in the middle to see the river, the ships, and the varied shores.

At the New York anchorage a U-shaped concrete block pulls each main cable with a tension of 62 million pounds. Cables are carried to saddles atop each steel tower, some

Wikimedia Commons

600 feet above the river. Each saddle rests on a flatbed on which 41 8-inch-diameter steel rollers distribute the load of the bridge to the tower columns.

At night the bridge is lit up, a fantasy of twinkling jewels above the river. From atop the tower near the New York shore, a beacon sweeps 50 miles of night sky.

In 1868, the New Jersey legislature authorized a Hudson River bridge while John Roebling was building the Brooklyn Bridge. Hundreds of designs were devised during the next 60 years. It was not until October 21, 1927, that ground breaking took place on both sides of the river and construction began. Othmar Ammann, a brilliant Swiss engineer, designed and oversaw construction of the bridge for the Port Authority of New York and New Jersey. The structure was completed and opened to grand fanfare by Franklin Roosevelt, then governor of New York, in October 1931. It cost about $60 million to build. The second, lower level was opened in 1963.

A pedestrian toll of 10 cents was in force at the opening; the bus across charged 5 cents. The bridge has made an enormous amount of money ever since. To cross from Jersey to New York by car cost $8 in 2011; the passage to New Jersey is free. Some 85 million vehicles traverse the bridge annually.

Though bicyclists were initially supposed to use only the north walkway, many use the south way since it has no steps up that one must lug a bike. I have no strong preference; both walkways offer delights to the eye and spirit. On each, incomparable views of the river and its shore greet the bridge walker. On a clear day, one can see the Statue of Liberty and Staten Island, the majestic mass of midtown skyscrapers to the southeast, and the high-rise buildings on the Jersey side.

Looking northwest, one sees the unbroken sweep of the vertically rising Palisades covered with green in the warmer months; red, yellow, and gold in the fall; gray-brown and sometimes snow-white in the winter.

Christine Yost

To the northeast lies Riverdale, the richest neighborhood of the Bronx; the towns of Yonkers, Hastings, and Tarrytown; as well as smaller riverine Westchester villages. The Tappan Zee Bridge crosses the river to the north between Tarrytown and Nyack, which, to its builders' shame, does not provide a walkway for pedestrians. This must be changed when voters demand New York State treat its bipeds with greater dignity and expand greenways.

A train sweeping down from the north moves along the Bronx shore like a shiny eel. Though running at 60 miles per hour or more, from our midbridge view, the train seems to crawl along the Hudson's edge.

◀ *View of sailboats on the Hudson River, with New Jersey and the George Washington Bridge in the distance*

After half an hour or so on the bridge (the time depending on how long you spend gazing at the varied and gorgeous scenery), exit onto New Jersey soil.

Exit the bridge from the south ramp by walking past the bus stop, then veering south on an exit ramp to River Road. Then turn north and walk under the bridge ramp to the entrance to the Palisades Interstate Park atop the Palisades. Exiting from the bridge's north ramp is less complicated: At the western end of the bridge, on the right, one can enter the park directly through a door in a chain-link fence. Listen! When you walk 200 yards into the dense woods atop the Palisades, notice the sharp drop in noise from the 16 lanes of bridge traffic.

From Bridge Plaza in Fort Lee it is worth an hour or more to veer south to the Fort Lee Historical Museum (201-768-1360), where America's

▼ *Rustic walk, Fort Lee Park, Hudson River, ca. 1888*

Wikimedia Commons/Continent Stereoscopic Company

Revolutionary history is displayed in dioramas, costumes, and written explanations. When we visited Fort Lee one May, a group of citizens dressed up as Civil War soldiers were holding an encampment. They marched in battle dress, took commands from their officers, and fired off a deafening volley of rifle shells. Wooden bunkhouses, tents, and realistic encampments were set up around the museum. In 1776, from the heights of Fort Lee, General Washington watched the British haul down the 13-starred U.S. flag from Fort Washington across the river. Fort Lee stands as a vivid reminder of U.S. Revolutionary history along the Hudson.

In October one may see flocks of gray geese in tight V formation, wings close to the water, flying rapidly south . . . a red-tailed hawk floating through the sky eyeing the river and the rocks below . . . poison ivy leaves along the cliff's shore painting the rocks bright red. Suddenly a rainbow appears, with one end in the Hudson north of the bridge—a bright spectrum hovering above—and the other end a red-orange-yellow-green-blue stripe descending into the canyons of midtown Manhattan.

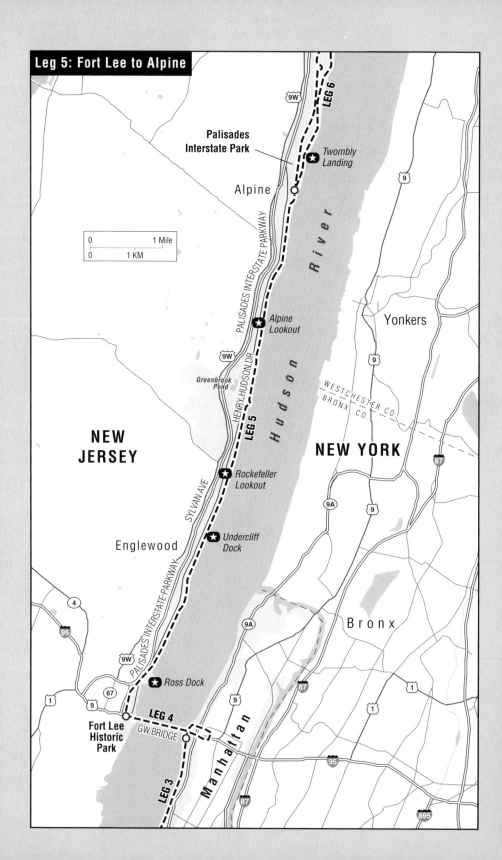

Leg 5: Fort Lee to Alpine

Palisades
Interstate Park

Twombly
Landing

9W

LEG 6

Alpine

PALISADES INTERSTATE PARKWAY

River

Yonkers

9

Alpine
Lookout

9W

HENRY HUDSON DR.

Greenbrook
Pond

LEG 5

Hudson

WESTCHESTER CO.
BRONX CO.

9

NEW
JERSEY

NEW YORK

87

Rockefeller
Lookout

SYLVAN AVE

9A

9

Undercliff
Dock

Englewood

PALISADES INTERSTATE PARKWAY

Bronx

4

9A

87

95

9

1

9W

1

67

Ross Dock

9

9

Fort Lee
Historic
Park

LEG 4

1

GW BRIDGE

Manhattan

95

LEG 3

87

895

0   1 Mile
0   1 KM

LEG 5

FORT LEE TO ALPINE

ABOUT 7 MILES ALONG THE SHORE

Walk aside with me. I have studied eight or nine wise words to speak with you.

—*William Shakespeare*

A sudden sweet silence descends on the walker when coming off the George Washington Bridge into the woods on top of the Palisades.

Legs 5 and 6 of the Hudson River Shore Trail can be walked in one fell swoop of about 12 miles from the New Jersey side of the great bridge to the New York state line. However, here we break this unique shore walk into two shorter segments: Leg 5, Fort Lee to Alpine, about 7 miles; and Leg 6, Alpine to the State Line, about 4–5 miles.

Car drivers, take note: No cars are allowed to drive along this section of the Hudson River Shore Trail for most of its 12 miles. Automobiles can be parked year-round at several lots in the Palisades Interstate Park, however. Car lots exist at Fort Lee Historic Park, at the Englewood-Bloomers Boat Basin, and at the Alpine Area Boat Basin.

Walkers crossing the George Washington Bridge, or taking the Red and Tan bus from terminals in Manhattan, can leave (or catch) a bus at the west end of the bridge, at Alpine (Closter Dock Road), or at the state line. Buses run approximately once every hour; for current schedules and fares, go to www.coachusa.com/redandtan.

Exit the soaring bridge and walk north from Fort Lee's condominiums, which jut from the top of the cliffs like bad teeth. Walk through the quiet woods of the Palisades Interstate Park atop the Palisades, but not too close to the edge of the sheer cliffs; a fall will likely cause death. After a short walk of about about 10 minutes through the woods, we encounter the Carpenter's Trail, a zigzag flight of about 400 stone steps hewn into the cliff.

Carefully descend more than 400 feet on the winding granite staircase etched into the vertical cliff to reach the shore of the Hudson River. This exhilarating descent provides beautiful, ever-changing vistas of the river, the great bridge, and the New York shore. The hewn stone steps and much of the trail were built by the Civilian Conservation Corps (CCC) during the 1930s.

The sinuous shore path undulates over rocks, tree stumps, and vines, through mud hollows and sands, following the Hudson water's edge most of the way. One hears and sees waves breaking on the rocks in this estuary, which here is about three quarters of a mile wide. A strong east wind can churn up respectable waves; speeding motor vessels send waves to bounce against the rocky shores and shallow beaches. Old stumps, pilings, and large logs sometimes are washed up on the shore; tides of 5 to 6 feet rise and fall here twice a day. Fifty miles upriver in the vicinity of Bear Mountain, the diurnal tides average 2.5 feet; 150 miles north

▶ *Walking south in New Jersey along the Hudson River, with the George Washington Bridge in view*

Christine Yost

of the Battery, the tidal waves break feebly against the federal dam at Troy.

Often the shorewalker comes upon anglers and crabbers trying their luck. More sports anglers have appeared since the late 1980s as the Hudson's waters became cleaner. This very noticeable increase in water quality is due to sharper surveillance by concerned citizens, a decrease in industrial activity along the river, stronger antipollution laws, and, not incidentally, the expenditure of more than $40 billion on new sewage treatment plants since the 1960s. Hudson River waters in 2011 are clean enough to swim in.

In the spring, a handful of local Jersey commercial fishermen string gill nets attached to poles stuck in the river's muddy bottom to snag shad as they swim in from the ocean and up the Hudson to spawn. These shad fishermen are the remnants of several families who have been gill-netting shad for hundreds of years. In the 1990s, shad fishermen complained that their nets were being torn up by schools of voracious, healthy bass

swimming up the Hudson to spawn. The bass could not legally be taken as food fish because they had traces of PCBs in their livers. (Pete Seeger and I put together a little song.)

Song of the Happy Hudson Bass

Swift, fat bass fresh from the sea,
Let us all praise PCB
Dumped upstream by rich GE
So that we can swim free.

Swim on, swim on, swim on, swift bass,
May you all swim on.

In the Hudson we increase,
Multiply without surcease
Grow fat in bights and bays;
Stripers, these are glory days!

Swim on, swim on, swim on, swift bass,
May you all swim on.

As long as people fear to eat
Our tasty, sweet, and juicy meat
We hunt the Hudson alive,
Gorge smaller fish and thrive.

Swim on, swim on, swim on, swift bass,
May you all swim on.

So stripers bless PCB
It saved the skins of you and me,
May traces long be found
So we're not broiled, fried, or ground.

Swim on, swim on, swim on, swift bass,
May you all swim on.

Music by Pete Seeger
Words by Cy A Adler

Shad is an oily, tasty fish. Its spawning run up the Hudson gives rise to shad bakes along the river in which fish are nailed to a wooden plank, covered with strips of bacon, and baked over hot coals. Delicious! Shad roe is another local delicacy.

Fort Lee to the Englewood-Bloomers Boat Basin is a walk of approximately 3 flat miles. Before the bridge was built, ferries carried New Yorkers from Dyckman Street and 125th Street to this ample dock. Walking north along the level, sinuous footpath, we pass the Ross Dock, where one finds picnic facilities and, in the warmer months, refreshments. There are several good spots for fishing, and bathrooms are available as well, as is parking. The narrow sandy shore path winds north below the Palisades for 1.5 miles, opening up to the Englewood-Bloomers public boat basin. Here one can park a car. Clean toilets and water can be found here, as well as snacks during June and July.

In May sweet smelling blossoms, flowering dogwood, lilacs, columbines, and violets, among other, less common plants, line the path. In spring and summer heavy foliage, grapevines, trees, bushes, flowers, and grasses surround this virtually flat, sinuous shore trail. In the winter, cold and icy weather attracts fewer people—but there's greater quiet.

Hikers sometimes carry plastic bags to pick up trash that other, thoughtless humans have dropped. But, in general, the shore trail is relatively litter free. This contrasts with walking trails along roadways where passing motorists may contribute bottles, cans, plastic, and rubber goods to the natural environment.

Black long-necked gannets and other water birds have come back to the cleaner river in recent years. And gulls, survivors and smarter than most other birds. I smile, watch, listen to, and wonder at these graceful birds. Some humans sneer at gulls as brash scavengers of trash. Effortlessly, sweepingly, they soar through the air, sometimes quacking to each other as they fly. In all seasons one is also likely to encounter ducks, noisy crows, and Canada geese. In spring, a wide variety of exotic migrating birds fly in from the south. Red-tailed hawks glide high above, patrolling the sky.

Walk past the remnants of abandoned rock quarries. From the 17th to 19th centuries, builders and contractors from New York and New Jersey blasted and chipped away billions of tons of rock from the vertical cliffs, tumbled the stone down to the water's edge, and then barged it to city docks to build streets, bridges, brownstones, and multistory dwellings.

From Englewood Boat Basin to Alpine Landing, the path abuts the river for about 5.5 miles. The shore path dips and wallows in spots that flood after heavy downpours. Walkers have also been cut off at high tides and must scamper on the rocks and/or wet their shoes. I suggest you take the higher bypass.

Tread carefully to avoid the poison ivy growing in profusion in patches along the trail. In warm, wet years the ivy blooms in great abundance. Park managers wrote me that their budget was cut and they did not have adequate staff to clear the weed. Walkers should wear long-sleeved shirts and trousers.

About 3 miles north of the Englewood-Bloomers dock, we pass close to Buttermilk Falls, whose waters originate above, in the Greenbrook Sanctuary. These almost vertical falls are spectacular after heavy rains. After a heavy downpour, tons of water cascade down the sheer cliffs in a magnificent display. A dry month later there will be hardly a trickle down the gray rocks. This example of nature's fickleness calls to mind a verse from Peter Agnos: "Capricious Nature makes honey and fills honey carts, / Causes lilacs to bloom and makes elephant farts. / Nature decrees all life must go to pot; / From day to day we ripen; from day to day we rot."

On this winding shore trail, one must climb through the woods up an incline of about 100 feet at several locations. Scattered along the way are a few rough stone tables with hewn stone benches made of blocks of igneous rock. A delightful spot to have lunch is the stone assemblage near the Buttermilk Waterfall.

After climbing down the Carpenters Trail from atop the Palisades in Fort Lee, the shorewalker has only one exit at Englewood-Bloomers Boat Basin before reaching the Alpine boat docks 8 miles north of the George Washington Bridge.

Twice a day salty tidal water flows into the wide, placid Hudson estuary from the Atlantic to help purify and freshen it. Upriver, 30 miles or so, in the vicinity of Poughkeepsie the river is fresh enough to drink. Between the river's mouth and Poughkeepsie, the saltier, colder ocean water sinks below the fresher upstate water to form a saltwater wedge, with denser tidal waters underlying fresh water from upstream.

Near the shore, two gulls cry as they circle over a near-shore patch of marsh grass. It sounds not so much like a cry, but a complaint, a long lament, full toned and intense. These gulls' contralto cries carry far over the water, then fade away. An echo sounds. A walker also often encounters Canada geese, which sometimes bark like dogs. Natural sounds are more audible and intense along the Hudson River Shore Trail away from motors, wheels, and radios. Alas, a few motorboaters rend the air with their cacophonous noises, which drown out the gulls' lament.

▶ *The rocky shore path north of the Englewood Boat Basin*

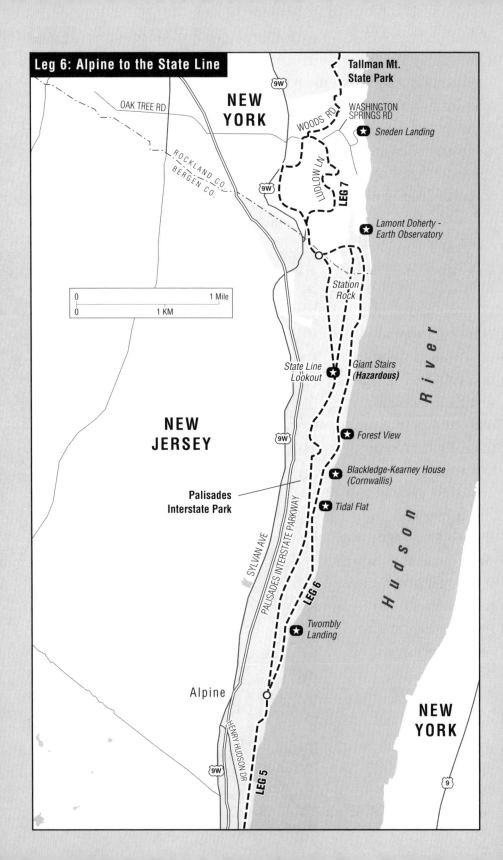

Leg 6: Alpine to the State Line

NEW YORK

Tallman Mt. State Park

OAK TREE RD

9W

WOODS RD

WASHINGTON SPRINGS RD

★ Sneden Landing

ROCKLAND CO.
BERGEN CO.

9W

LUDLOW LN

LEG 7

★ Lamont Doherty - Earth Observatory

Station Rock

0   1 Mile
0   1 KM

NEW JERSEY

9W

State Line Lookout

★ Giant Stairs (*Hazardous*)

River

Hudson

★ Forest View

★ Blackledge-Kearney House (Cornwallis)

★ Tidal Flat

Palisades Interstate Park

SYLVAN AVE

PALISADES INTERSTATE PARKWAY

LEG 6

★ Twombly Landing

Alpine

HENRY HUDSON DR

9W

LEG 5

NEW YORK

9

LEG 6

ALPINE TO THE STATE LINE

ABOUT 4–5 MILES OF UNDULATING SHORE TRAIL FOLLOWED BY WICKED ROCKS AND A STEEP CLIMB OF 400 FEET

There is an inward voice, that in
the stream
Sends forth its spirit to the
listening ear,
And in calm content it floweth on.
Like wisdom, welcome with its
own respect,
Clear in its breast lie all these
beauteous thoughts,
It doth receive the green and
graceful trees,
And the gray rocks smile in its
peaceful arms.

from "The River" by
William Ellery Channing

The Alpine Boat Basin at the foot of the Palisade cliffs has facilities for docking boats and for parking cars. Drivers may enter from Palisades Parkway or US 9W at the cloverleaf directly north of Closter Dock Road, which runs east–west. Hikers may park here year-round. Atop the Palisades, nearby in Alpine, is a lookout more than 500 feet above the river-level path. One can see Manhattan, the Bronx, and Long Island embedded in their estuaries.

Pedestrians who wish to exit from the shore trail at this point may take the stony winding path that leads more than 400 feet up to Closter Dock Road, where one can catch a Red and Tan bus back to the George Washington Bridge or to 42nd Street in Manhattan. Buses run about once every hour during the day. The stony path starts immediately north of the Blackledge-Kearney house and is marked by a historical plaque: The British marched up this path in 1776 in their attempt to catch George Washington and his fleeing rebels. George was too fast for them.

At the Alpine marina the hiker can find water, snacks, and toilets in the summertime. Just north of the boat basin is the famous Blackledge-Kearney house, an old, white two-and-a-half-story house that, local legend

long maintained, served as General Cornwallis's temporary headquarters during the Revolutionary War. The stone and wood house was built about 1750. In December 1991 we found the front door ajar; we entered cautiously. No one was around. We climbed to the second story of the building and wandered through a unique miniature colonial museum. A furnished bedroom upstairs contained a dummy of a woman in a large Colonial hat. We took pictures and commented to each other that this historical building and its contents could easily be vandalized.

In June 1993 I was delighted to find the house guarded by a troop of redcoats—seven men and a boy, all in black, cocked hats; bright red jackets; mustard-yellow sashes and breeches. Four triangular, 17th-century army tents pitched on the front lawn were tended by two women dressed in Colonial garb. The men marched in two's and then four's, accompanied by a lively fifer, attended by the small boy diligently carrying a wooden rifle. At their captain's command the men "wheeled right," stopped at "company halt," lifted their large, clumsy rifles at "present arms," and discharged their muskets at "fire," making a big bang.

As of May 2011, the house is open May through October, on weekends and holidays between noon and 5 PM. To learn more details, call 201-768-1360, ext. 108, or go to www.njpalisades.org/kearney.

◀ *Cy Adler walking north from Alpine on the Batt to Bear Trail.*

Christine Yost

Just south and in front of the old house with its peeling white paint is a large, cubical rock. This black chunk of basalt, about 8 feet high, fell off the Palisades cliffs in 1896 and rolled onto the attached kitchen, which it completely demolished. Assuming the rock is thrice the density of water, this slight chip off the Palisades weighs more than 70,000 pounds.

From Alpine north to Forest View is about 2.5 miles as the seagull flies, longer when one hikes along the winding shore. This section of the trail climbs and veers inland a few hundred feet, but one can always see the majestic Hudson River through the trees. There is no way to leave the trail hereabouts—to the west sheer cliffs rise more than 400 feet, to the east flows the river. Here nature is most beautiful as the wind murmurs through the trees to the river. Along the path, glimpse magnificent vistas of the river and the railroad towns on the opposite shore. Rampant growth entwines virtually every inch of the narrow way; on either side: vines wrap trees; small, white wild roses bloom in June; poison ivy grows, alas; and yellow, red, and blue wildflowers flourish.

Rounding a bend in the river, I thought I heard a dog barking. "*Bark! Bark!*" Moving farther north, I spied a large Canada goose standing on a grassy promontory in the river and honking very much like a large dog. A quarter of a mile farther north, a family of four large Canada geese and four goslings swam near the shore. These big, beautiful, but dirty honkers, sometimes called ringnecks or blacknecks, showed no inclination for migrating back to Canada. *Branta canadensis* feed on ground and water plants. They weigh 5 to 9 pounds. The smaller female incubates five or six creamy-white eggs while the gander hangs around to protect and help rear the brood. These handsome geese are smart, aggressive birds . . . I have been told one can find them in Montreal, smoked.

Walk through a heavily wooded area where in June the foliage makes it difficult to see either the cliffs to the west or the river to the east. The shore path is usually well marked by white rectangular blazes.

◀ *Pete Nekola walking north from Alpine*

Christine Yost

At the bottom of the cliffs one finds sections of red sandstone, above which jut vertical columns of gray brownstone. The sedimentary red stone is embedded in thousand-foot-thick layers of shale, consolidated sand, and mud, all compressed for 200 million years. Through these layers intruded molten rocks, formed some 190 million years ago. The softer sandstone crumbled and weathered away over the ages, leaving a single, continuous sill called the Palisades. They are about 1,000 feet thick in some places and run about 40 miles north to south along the Hudson coast of New Jersey and New York.

Across the river is much older Precambrian rock, on which rest Yonkers and Manhattan. The Hudson River cuts through the cleavage between the old New York rock and the younger New Jersey formation. The narrow shore fields below the cliffs were heavily farmed by the Dutch for more than a hundred years. They called this fertile strip "under the mountain," and that it still is. The Hudson provided a natural means of transportation, forests atop the Palisades provided timber and firewood, and Palisades stone provided building matter.

After the Civil War these enormous rock cliffs were in danger of being reduced to rubble and paving stones, and barged away by quarry operators. Men blasted the cliffs to obtain crushed stone for street paving and for construction in the booming New York metropolitan area, and for the growing towns on the route of New York State's great watery artery to America's west, the Erie Canal. A group of wealthy and concerned citizens who lamented the almost certain demise of the Palisades formed the Palisades Commission of New York and New Jersey. While the states contributed $15,000, J. P. Morgan, the mathematics student turned financier; John D. Rockefeller Jr., son of the man called by Senator Robert Lafollette and others "the greatest thief of his era"; and other eminent tycoons threw in a few hundred thousand dollars to buy the remaining quarries in the 1890s. George W. Perkins deserves special mention as the commission's first president and organizing genius. Fortunately for the Palisades, no income tax bothered the wealthy tycoons in those days. By 1900 the rock blasting had ceased. Smaller land purchases were later made atop the cliffs, and in 1909 the Palisades Interstate Park (PIP) opened for visitors. In New Jersey, PIP runs from Fort Lee at its south end to the New York state border—about 13 miles as the crow flies—and then in New York covers Tallman State Park, High Tor, and Bear Mountain Park. As I walk I give thanks to the turn-of-the-20th-century "robber baron" philanthropists for their foresight in creating the PIP and for having donated some of their loot to preserving the Palisades. Today, the PIP Commission owns some 2,500 acres in New Jersey and more than 78,000 acres in New York State. From Forest View to the state line is about 2 rugged miles, a mostly up-and-down climb to the top of the 500-foot cliffs. This final section of the shore path in New Jersey is most striking and strenuous; do not expect to make it in less than two hours. Because of the immense jagged boulders and broken rocks, no cars or bicycles come this way. This visually and physically exhilarating trail should be attempted open by serious, well-prepared hikers.

One must traverse the slide and talus carefully, stepping only on solid rock. This little-trod wilderness is not a good place to walk alone, or to twist an ankle. Copperheads, rattlers, and black snakes, as well as intrepid hikers, crawl this rocky area. If alone and bitten, creep to the guard booth at the state line to call for help.

Heading north, pick your way rock by rock along a jagged creviced path for about a mile, then walk another half mile close to the shore. Pass over a slough that divides New Jersey from New York. This section of the trail is called the Summit Walk. Along the river are projections into the Hudson: Morrow Point, Moss Rock, and High Gutter Point. Here, the remains of earlier industrial activities still jut into the river.

One must climb a rock stairway known as the Stairway to the Sun—or, more commonly, the Giant's Stairs—to Gellhorn Point, where the trail forks. Shun the Middle Way Trail, going west, and take the northerly Dickenson Trail along the shore to a promontory called Lover's Ledge on some romantic maps, Peanut Leap on more prosaic charts. Here, a narrow stream empties over a waterfall (the Corliss Cascades) into the Hudson River.

Near the path lie the ruins of what was once an elaborate grape arbor. A local fellow told me that this spot was hereabouts called the Guinea's Garden in honor of the wealthy Italian who once had an estate here. Most likely this was an estate owned by Lydia G. Lawrence, who modeled the structure and garden on one she saw in Amalfi, a rocky Italian seaside town. She willed the property to the PIP Commission in the early 1900s. Vines and wild plants cover everything except several cracked concrete columns protruding from the weedy ground.

A few words of caution: Negotiating the rocks in this region requires strong, sturdy boots; excellent balance; the ability to jump from rock to rock; and steady nerves. Clambering here should only be attempted in good light and with healthy companions. One of Shorewalkers' early intrepid leaders, although, tried scouting this section alone late on a fall Sunday afternoon. She was halfway up when the sun dipped west over the cliffs, leaving the area in semidarkness. Afraid of missing her step, twisting an ankle, and falling off the rocky path in the dark, she huddled on a damp rock all night in the chill air. She shivered in the dark till rosy-fingered dawn crept up over Long Island. Wet and disheveled, she caught a Red and Tan commuter bus, startling several New York City–bound executives.

At the New York–New Jersey state line, citizen shorewalkers can proceed no farther north along the river since Columbia University has fenced their property here. Columbia maintains the Lamont-Doherty Earth Observatory (LDEO), one of the leading geological and oceanographic centers in the world. Once it was the estate of botanist John Torrey, and then of Corliss Lamont, who gave it to Columbia. This private, nonprofit, educational organization does not allow citizens to walk along the river— which by common consent belongs to all and should be accessible to the public. A more public-spirited administration may change this policy. In passing we note that both New Jersey and New York have laws that protect landowners who provide environmental easements through their property from liability suits arising from use of these easements.

The walker must take the west fork path along the Lamont sanctuary fence, up a well-trod path to where the Masefield-Lamont Trail meets a spur on the right near a small stream. Continue through Skunk Hollow over land owned by Columbia University along a short spur. This carries the walker to the guarded entrance of the Lamont Doherty grounds, and to US 9W. The guardhouse is manned 24 hours a day and has a first-aid and snakebite kit. At the junction of the hiking path, and the road into LDGO, one can catch a Red and Tan bus on US 9W to the George Washington Bridge Bus Terminal in upper Manhattan or to the Port Authority Bus Terminal at 42nd Street. The carborne can find limited parking facilities in this area. A varied and beautiful hiking path on top of the Palisades lies ahead.

If a walker calls in advance, Lamont usually will give permission to walk along the main road through the facility. (Their phone number is 845-359-2900; visit their website at www.ldeo.columbia.edu.) We thank Lamont for being very accommodating in allowing Shorewalkers to hike through on Leg 7.

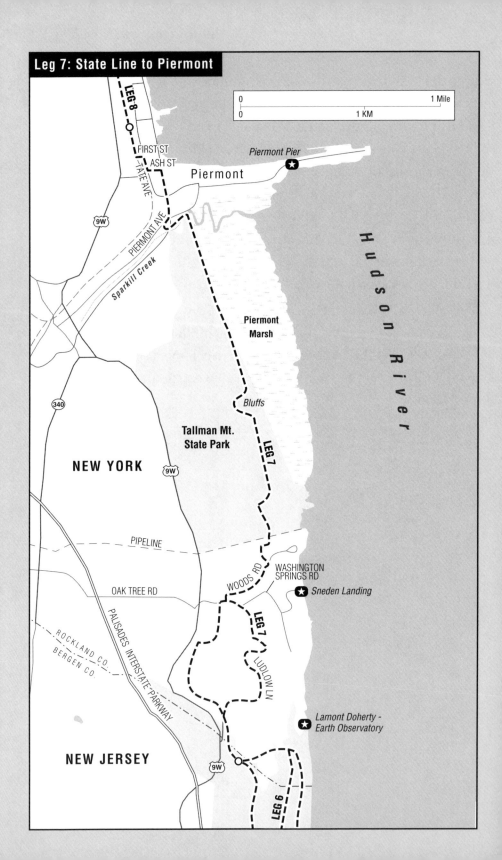

Leg 7: State Line to Piermont

LEG 8

FIRST ST
ASH ST

Piermont

Piermont Pier ★

STATE AVE

US 9W

PIERMONT AVE

Sparkill Creek

Piermont Marsh

Bluffs

Tallman Mt. State Park

NY 340

US 9W

NEW YORK

LEG 7

Hudson River

PIPELINE

WOODS RD

WASHINGTON SPRINGS RD

OAK TREE RD

★ *Sneden Landing*

LEG 7

LUDLOW LN

ROCKLAND CO.
BERGEN CO.

PALISADES INTERSTATE PARKWAY

★ *Lamont Doherty - Earth Observatory*

NEW JERSEY

US 9W

LEG 6

0 ——————————— 1 Mile
0 ——————————— 1 KM

LEG 7

STATE LINE TO PIERMONT

ABOUT 3 MILES FROM THE RIDGE OF THE PALISADES TO SEA LEVEL

Blowing in the breeze
of the floating universe
weeds drift here and there.

—*K. Issa*

◄ *We usually go through the main north-south road of Lamont Doherty Observatory, then take Washington Springs Road to Wood Road, then go west a short way to Iron Grill gate, then north along the unmarked wooded path to Tallman Mt. State Park.*

From the New York–New Jersey state line to Piermont village is about 3 miles, which should take about an hour of steady walking. But allot at least two hours to enjoy the great views of the woods and marshes, and the delights of Piermont.

Drivers can park either at the entrance to Tallman Park at US 9W north of Oak Tree Road, or in Piermont. The Red and Tan bus line can take walkers from the 178th Street Port Authority Terminal in Manhattan either to Oak Tree Road near the state line (in about 20 minutes) or to Piermont.

North of the New York–New Jersey state line, private landowners deny the shorewalker the pleasure of trailing along the water's edge. We trust this unfortunate deprivation of the public's right of innocent passage will be alleviated in the near future. Shorewalkers have scouted a

3-mile walking route skirting the existing trails. Our route has considerable natural charm as it wanders through woods and parkland.

After leaving the state line, walk north either through the Lamont-Doherty Earth Observatory or to the west of it, parallel to US 9W.

You can continue along 9W about a quarter mile till you come to a small parking lot, and take a dirt road on the right that leads into Tallman Mountain State Park. This is part of the Long Path, a major crest-top hiking path from the George Washington Bridge through the Catskill Mountains. To get off 9W, an unpleasant and hazardous truck road, walk east on Washington Springs Road (Old Oak Tree Road)

toward Sneden's (or Sneden on some maps) Landing.

I prefer walking north from the state line through the Lamont campus. One must first obtain permission by calling security at 845-365-8822. Formerly the grounds of Corlis Lamont, a rich robber baron, the beautiful campus is now a geological and oceanographic research center. Campus buildings house deep-sea cores and tree rings and biological contraptions. At its northern end is the library, which was, I believe, the main mansion. In front of it is an apple tree grove and a large statue of Lincoln reading while riding on a horse. On several occasions Lamont scientists invited us in to count the tree rings, which indicate past global warming/cooling trends, and to view the deep sea cores.

The northern unguarded exit of Lamont leads to quiet, winding Ludlow Lane. We pass few houses to the west, woods and views of the Hudson to the east. It leads to Washington Springs Road. To the east is Sneden's Landing; to the west, our route to Woods Road. We pass pretty Palisades Presbyterian, a Colonial-style church.

Sneden's Landing was the western end of a Hudson River ferry route started in the 18th century. According to local legend, during the Revolutionary War, Mollie Sneden, a Revolutionary sympathizer, smuggled

◀ *This route passes through woods.*

important secret messages to General Washington's troops. Her house still stands near the water's edge, surrounded by rich mansions. The British fleet used the anchorage from 1776 until Cornwallis surrendered.

◀ *The site of the original ferry landing on the Hudson River above New York City is known as Sneden's Landing.*

Wikimedia Commons/Hisland7

Continuing due east along Washington Springs's winding, sloping, asphalt road, in about 20 minutes you will arrive at a small, bare, stone landing-dock jutting into the Hudson, from which you can catch an impressive view of the river and the Tappan Zee Bridge. There's little else there for the walker to see. Sneden's Landing has become an enclave of big estates and expensive houses with no obvious public amenities—not even a stand for buying a Coke. The area is charmingly undemocratic.

On a fence around a spacious lawn, we saw a placard posted and dated October 3, 1990, that gave notice of a public meeting to discuss Mikhail Baryshnikov's plans for an addition to his existing Red Barn. In front of a massive three-story brick mansion on the Hudson decorated with manicured French poodles, a French-speaking gardener discouraged us from seeking the shore. Signs next to the dock that abuts the old Sneden House proclaim PRIVATE PROPERTY and NO TRESPASSING, leaving casual walkers with the impression they are not welcome.

To continue walking to Bear Mountain from Sneden's Landing, take Washington Springs Road east from 9W for a few minutes till you see a large two-story stone building on the left-hand side of the road fronted with a triangular green plot. Do not pass the church on the right. Veer north onto Woods Road, which winds through groves of large trees and goes by several large, handsome houses. This dead-end route is much more desirable for walking than busy 9W, a few hundred yards to the west.

Follow Woods Road, lined with 80-foot trees, for about a half mile till you come to a fork in the road and a large tree decorated with somewhat confusing signs, which on an expedition in the 1990s read HAAGENSENS, TAPLEYS, NO LARGE TRUCKS. Veer east toward the Hudson until you see a small footpath through the woods leading north. The path is near a lone, ornate, metal gate. If you see or hear several large dogs (hopefully penned behind a fence), you have taken the wrong fork.

Follow this narrow, wooded path north for about 500 feet. Continue to a clearing in the woods, the right-of-way for a buried gas pipeline, through which you can view the river. You are atop the Palisades on a bluff high above the Hudson shore. Beyond this clearing the path widens and soon intersects a bike path in Tallman Mountain State Park.

Most of Tallman Mountain State Park (845-359-0544; www.nysparks. com) lies on a 150- to 200-foot-high plateau south of the town of Piermont and north of Sneden's Landing. The PIP Commission acquired about 100 of the park's 687 acres in 1929. Subsequently, oil companies proposed building a gigantic tank farm and loading dock in the south part of the site. Public indignation killed the plan, and 540 acres were added to the park in 1942. The park has playing fields, a large bird population, toilets, and picnic areas. On warm Sundays, families drive in and fill the air with children's shouts; smells of barbecued meat and chicken greet one's nostrils near the broilers. Fortunately the park is large and wild enough to suit the most reclusive walker.

Walk east toward the river along the level and pretty bike path passing heavily wooded areas, rocky outcrops, and dirt berms about 6 feet high and perpendicular to the road. These berms were built by Standard Oil companies in the 1920s to contain potential oil spills from a proposed oil tank farm. Now large trees grow atop and beside the berms. The depressions between the berms fill with water after heavy rains. Water and foliage attract many birds. After walking a mile or so, the dirt road curves north and then comes to an extensive picnic area on a Tallman bluff—the North Picnic Ground. Here you will find cars, benches, and tables, and in the summer, toilets and water.

In addition, an unmarked path skirts the edge of the cliff, winding and undulating as it descends to a brook that is fordable except in times of heavy rain. This trail is less frequently used but is easily followed. One can spy through the trees the great green marsh, the Hudson, and the nether shore of Westchester. After half a mile this unblazed trail intersects the main bike path and trail, which is blazed blue. After about 15 minutes more of walking (half mile), one comes to a fork in the trail. Veer east to picnic tables and the stone outhouse (closed between Labor Day and Memorial Day).

From the bluff above the Hudson one can get a magnificent view of the Piermont Pier, overgrown with weeds and trees, and a tacky new housing development built in the 1990s on the pier head. The remainder of the mile-long pier jutting into the Hudson is undeveloped parkland overgrown with trees and shrubs. It is a great place to fish or watch for birds.

From the Tallman bluffs one can also observe the sinuous, walkway-less Tappan Zee Bridge, the Hudson's eastern shore north of Yonkers, and to the south, the rectangular skyscrapers of New York City.

We walk north from the stone buildings that house the comfort stations by a road that exits Tallman Park down to the Piermont Marsh. Walk along the marsh to Sparkhill Creek at the southern end of Piermont Village. Here Sparkhill Creek flows into the Hudson. Cross the small bridge to Paradise Avenue into the village hugging the river.

To the east lies Piermont Marsh, the vast reed forest where 12-foot-high phragmites wave in the wind, their rhizomes matted in the trapped river muck. It was, in part, created unwittingly by Erie railroad engineers in the 1840s when they built the mile-long railroad pier due east into the river to reach the Hudson's deep channel.

Natural sedimentation caused by eddies in the

◀ *A winter view of Piermont, looking north from the mile-long Piermont Pier.*

Christine Yost

lee of the pier deposited billions of tons of rich silt on the floor of the river. Plants sprung up, and the man-made marsh grew willy-nilly. It attracted marine life, birds, and water-loving mammals. Meandering inlets cut through the dense marsh and phragmites grasses. In spring the foliage sports a delicate, shimmering pale green. Due to the many birds and marine animals, the marsh is a breeding place for myriads of fish. All a byproduct of technology. Part of the Hudson River National Estuarine Research Reserve, the 1,000-acre brackish, salty marsh is managed by the New York State Department of Environmental Conservation (845-889-4745; www.dec.ny.gov), and it can be visited by canoe or kayak (rentable in Piermont). The marsh is fragile—carry out what you carry in.

A detour out on the mile-long pier jutting into the Hudson is well worth the walk. The pier was constructed by the Erie Railroad Company in 1841 as its eastern-terminus transshipment point for seagoing vessels. Steamboats carried upstaters from here to downtown Manhattan. It was used extensively during the Second World War. In 1852 the Erie Company bought the rail line from Suffern to Jersey City, thus reducing the need for the Piermont terminus. More direct rail routes, the Container Revolution, the rise in use of petroleum-powered vehicles, and perhaps lack of a good European war forced discontinuance of the pier as a rail terminal. After 1950 it fell into disuse, its buildings lost windows and roofs, grass and weeds sprouted along the main roadways, and the rails rusted. In the late 1980s its rails were torn up, and in the 1990s the aforementioned housing development, called Paradise, was built on the pier.

Most of the once-extensive railroad lines in the shore area lie rusting or have been ripped up. An

▶ *Looking north from Piermont Pier to Palisades of Tallman Mt. Park*

Wikimedia Commons/Jim Henderson

important exception is the single-track Conrail line along the west shore, the main freight line from the north into the New Jersey metropolitan area. Environmental concerns, the rising price of gasoline, and a better-educated public may bring back commuter trains to supplant wasteful, polluting, automotive travel. Meanwhile, nature has recaptured the unused track beds and converted the shallows south of the pier into the rich, fertile Piermont Marsh.

Attractive, solidly built, old brick houses line Piermont's narrow side streets and congested roads running parallel to the Hudson. On a bright Sunday, a parade of cars slowly cruises down Piermont Avenue. Smartly attired strollers wander in and out of shops, or sip drinks at the sidewalk cafés; bikers in skin-hugging gear pedal along the narrow, two-lane main drag. One can find excellent food, coffee, beer, and sweets on Piermont Avenue or in the new stores and cafés on the pier. Boondocks (845-365-2221), an environmental boutique, sells books; several antiques shops cater to collectors. This yuppified former mill town provides a pleasant stop on the walk to Bear Mountain.

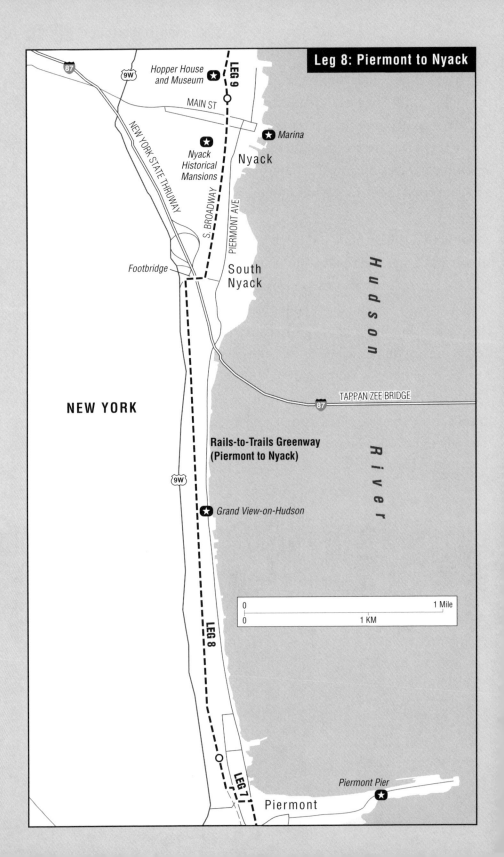

Leg 8: Piermont to Nyack

87
9W

Hopper House and Museum ★

LEG 9

MAIN ST

NEW YORK STATE THRUWAY

★ Marina

Nyack Historical Mansions ★

Nyack

S. BROADWAY

PIERMONT AVE

Footbridge

South Nyack

Hudson

TAPPAN ZEE BRIDGE
87

NEW YORK

Rails-to-Trails Greenway (Piermont to Nyack)

River

9W

★ Grand View-on-Hudson

| 0 | | 1 Mile |
| 0 | 1 KM | |

LEG 8

Piermont Pier ★

LEG 7

Piermont

LEG 8 | PIERMONT TO NYACK

THREE MILES OF QUIET WALKING
ALONG AN ABANDONED RAILROAD, OR
ALONG THE SHORE ROAD

The caged bird glances

with envy at the frail

but free butterfly.

—*K. Issa*

An excellent example of a newly
created walking greenway can be
found between the Hudson shore
villages of Piermont and Nyack.
This leg of the Batt to Bear Trail was
developed by local communities
from an abandoned commuter
railroad line. Though railway buffs
have floated the idea of reconverting
this greenway to an electric light
rail service, the chances of this
happening are remote. Many
environmentalists hope a passenger
rail line will again run along the
west bank of the Hudson. This can
be accomplished, in my opinion, by
using the existing Conrail water-level
track, which now carries only freight.

One can walk from Piermont to
Nyack along four different routes.
The first and most obvious walkway,
and the one closest to the Hudson,
is to continue north on Piermont
Avenue, which becomes River
Road. Follow busy River Road using

the narrow sidewalks, through Piermont and Grand View-on-Hudson. Many pretty houses and several beautiful mansions line the road. Private dwellings hug the Hudson shore most of the way, obscuring the walker's direct contact with—and sight of—the river. On this stretch only one small, unmarked riverside park can be found, in Grand View. Buses and cars traverse River Road, somewhat diminishing its charm as a walkway.

The second route is US 9W, with its nonexistent shoulder and dangerous speeding traffic. I would not recommend US 9W for pedestrians.

Thirdly, one can walk the Long Path route of about 7.5 miles, which starts out on 9W. From 9W switch to Highland (Tweed) Avenue until you reach Rockland Cemetery, a pretty and historic place. Then walk north on a ridge zigzagging to Nyack. This circuitous but well-marked route is for those hikers who enjoy clambering up and down ridges.

In 1986 a band of Shorewalkers discovered the fourth way to Nyack via an unmarked, shaded greenway. The Batt to Bear Trail goes along this abandoned commuter railroad right-of-way (ROW), which has been converted into a pleasant walkway by the three local communities along its path. From the early part of the 20th century until 1959, a branch line of the Erie Railroad carried commuters along this route from Nyack and other river communities to Jersey City, then by ferry to New York City. The rise of the automobile and changing living patterns doomed most American commuter railroad lines. This route's right-of-way was bought by the

communities of Piermont, Grand View, and Nyack, whose citizens opted to convert it to a linear park.

One can reach the unmarked converted rail ROW from Piermont Avenue in Piermont by zigzagging up Ash Street: right (north) on Tate Street, then west (left) on First Street. Streets are marked, but no arrow points the way. After a winding climb, one enters a level, tree-lined dirt path. From here glimpse the Hudson to the east. The steep slope to the west is dotted with several large, attractive houses. On both sides of the path the land leading up to the Palisades is probably too steep for extensive development.

About a mile north of Piermont, along the path we come upon a 2-foot cement post inscribed J.C. 25. It probably has nothing to do with Jesus Christ; more likely it indicates that Jersey City is 25 miles south by rail.

▼ *The Tappan Zee Bridge, as seen from*
Rockefeller State Park Preserve   Wikimedia Commons/Nr belex

Midway along the greenway to Nyack we come upon lush growths of knotweed (kudzu), a Japanese import gone wild. The weed has taken over large patches of open woods, covering poles and smothering ground cover. It grows thick, more than 6 feet tall. Most of the trail still displays the diversity of a mature Eastern deciduous forest. It is shaded and cool in summer, golden in the fall, delightful in any season. This car-free path is the quietest, most pleasant way to walk from Nyack to Piermont.

The last half mile of the path to Nyack sports a series of exercise bars and racks. At the end of the walk along this path we come to South Nyack. A small city park at the end of path has toilet facilities and water. At the north end of the abandoned-railroad greenway, old and substantial houses line the main road to Nyack. The path ends at a steel footbridge into central Nyack. Below the bridge, a maze of concrete roads leads to the Tappan Zee Bridge.

The Tappan Zee Bridge connects the west shore of the Hudson with Tarrytown in Westchester. New York State built the bridge at this wide point of the Hudson to funnel traffic from the New York State Thruway to the metropolitan area.

The S-shaped Tappan Zee Bridge is about 4 miles long and a vital link of the New York Thruway. Channel clearance is 145 feet; the main towers are 293 feet above the water. The bridge bends west to the cantilever towers and then bends south to Tarrytown. Built for $60 million in the 1950s, this handsome bridge does not provide a path for pedestrians or bicyclists. This unfortunate omission can now be corrected at much greater expense. Plans are afoot to build another vehicular bridge paralleling the Tappan Zee. Instead of spending the money to demolish the Tappan Zee, I urge it be converted into a walking-biking greenway (as I state in my letter to the editor of the *New York Times*, which follows). As more and more Americans take to their feet, all bridges must be designed for humans who walk, skate, or bicycle, as well as for automobilists. Write to the Governor of New York, Executive Mansion, Albany, NY 12224, and implore him to make all Hudson River bridges accessible to all human-powered forms of transportation.

Tappan Zee as a Walkway
October 17, 2011
Editor, *New York Times*:

Using the old Tappan Zee Bridge as a walkway is a great idea. Its 3-mile length should not be a serious deterrent to most walkers—it should take most of them about an hour.

The TZ Bridge ties into the Batt to Bear Trail at Nyack and would allow walkers to saunter from there north to Bear Mountain, or south to the Battery in Manhattan by using the George Washington Bridge.

Demolishing the bridge would be not only costly, but environmentally foolish.

We support the proposal to reuse the span for walkers and bikers, and perhaps a monorail.

Cy A Adler
President, Shorewalkers Inc.
www.shorewalkers.org

North of the bridge in Nyack, we found neat old townhouses and beautiful churches. Stroll through Nyack either along South Broadway or on pleasant and quieter Piermont Avenue, closer to the river. Nyack is a picturesque commuter town that caters to tourists, artists, and antiques hunters. Several beautiful old mansions line the streets. Fancy restaurants,

▼ *Francis Augustus Silva (American, 1835– 1886).* The Hudson at the Tappan Zee, 1876. *Oil on canvas, 24 x 42 3/16 in. (61 x 107.1 cm). Brooklyn Museum.*

Wikimedia Commons/Wikipedia Loves Art participant "shooting_brooklyn"

gussied-up taverns, antiques shops, craft shops, psychedelic establishments, real estate dealers, and good bakeries line Broadway and Main Street. One can dine at an old-fashioned chop house on Broadway, enjoy a Greek restaurant on Main Street, or sample baked pies at several locations. Walkers can also check out the charming and diverse Pickwick Book Shop (845-358-9126) at 8 South Broadway. One can lodge at the Best Western (845-358-8100; www.bestwestern.com) located at 26 NY 59, about a dozen blocks west of Broadway Street. Several groups of Shorewalkers have put up here on our two-day walking trips from Fort Lee to Bear Mountain led by Buddy Levine. There is also a Super 8 (845-353-3880; www.super8.com) at 47 NY 59.

To get closer to the Hudson, walk a block east of Broadway to Nyack's Memorial Park, ideal for bird-watching. There is a butterfly sanctuary. (Call the Nyack Village Hall at 845-358-0548 for more information.) Nearby are public piers where one can lunch and watch local fisherfolk waiting for striped bass 18 inches or longer.

▶ *American realist painter Edward Hopper's birthplace is in Nyack.*

Wikimedia Commons/Ritzel

At 82 North Broadway, north of Main Street, the two-story clapboard Edward Hopper House Art Center (845-358-0774; www.hopperhouse.org) displays paintings and memorabilia of the famous Depression-era artist who lived there, as well as works of other artists. Nearby on the shore I have seen artists painting seascapes.

History buffs can take self-guided tours of the area. For more information, check out the website of the Historical Society of the Nyacks at www.nyackhistory.org. You can also get in touch with Rockland County Tourism (1-800-295-5723; www.rockland.org) or Friends of the Nyacks (845-358-4973; www.friendsofthenyacks.org).

After taking liquid refreshments on the Hudson piers, cruising Main Street, stopping at the Edward Hopper house, and dallying a bit in Nyack, we continue walking along North Broadway on the way to Bear Mountain.

Note: Red and Tan buses from New York City and Fort Lee stop on River Road at Piermont and at three stops on Broadway in Nyack. Hikers out for the day can catch the bus at the 178th Street PATH bus station, the PATH terminal at 42nd Street, or in Fort Lee. Drivers can park in Piermont near the pier, or in Nyack. A car trip to Piermont or Nyack from New York City should take less than an hour.

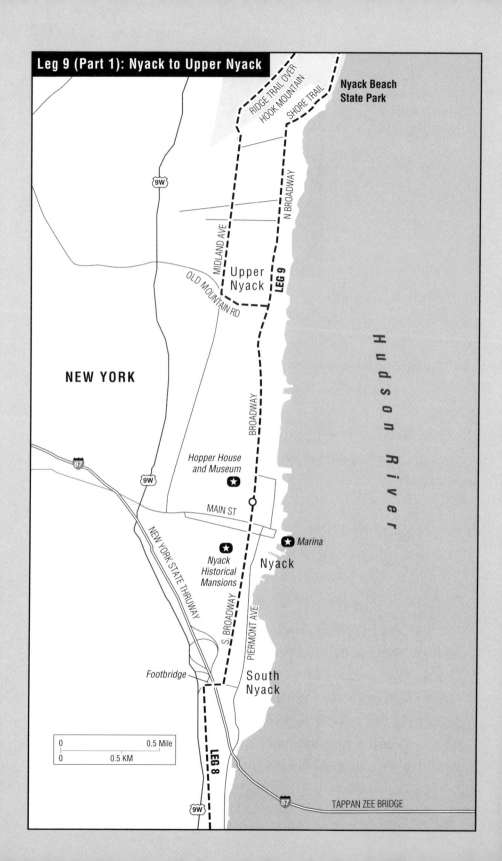

Leg 9 (Part 1): Nyack to Upper Nyack

Nyack Beach
State Park

RIDGE TRAIL OVER HOOK MOUNTAIN

SHORE TRAIL

9W

N BROADWAY

MIDLAND AVE

Upper
Nyack

LEG 9

OLD MOUNTAIN RD

NEW YORK

BROADWAY

Hudson River

87

9W

Hopper House
and Museum
★

MAIN ST

★ Marina

Nyack

Nyack
Historical
Mansions
★

NEW YORK STATE THRUWAY

S. BROADWAY

PIERMONT AVE

Footbridge

South
Nyack

LEG 8

0   0.5 Mile
0   0.5 KM

87   TAPPAN ZEE BRIDGE

9W

LEG 9

NYACK TO HAVERSTRAW

ABOUT 9.5 MILES ALONG THE SHORE, MOSTLY BELOW HOOK MOUNTAIN

Among all the rivers of the world the Hudson is acknowledged queen, decked with romance, jeweled with poetry, clad with history, and crowned with beauty. More than this, the Hudson is a noble threshold to a great continent and New York Bay a fitting portal.

—Wallace Bruce,
The Hudson, 1907

We walk this beautiful stretch in the shadow of Hook Mountain. It can be reached by car drivers if they park in Nyack State Park just north of Upper Nyack. However, the car driver who walks to Haverstraw may find no public transportation to return to his vehicle.

Hook Mountain looms north of the wealthy residential community of Upper Nyack. In Upper Nyack along Broadway, large, well-manicured spreads, big houses, and stately mansions stand between the walker and the river. Shadowcliff and Riverstrip are names given to two of these large mansions on extensive land sloping to the Hudson. Many of the estates are shielded from the street by high brick walls, thick wood fences, or privet hedges. In Upper Nyack, Broadway is the closest pedestrian street parallel to the Hudson. Several times while walking here during the 1980s, we saw sheep grazing on a vast, sloping lawn to the west of Broadway. No sheep were spotted in 2011, however. Famous actress Helen Hayes and several other notables lived hereabouts. Walking along quiet, shaded, and pleasant Broadway in Upper Nyack, one can occasionally glimpse the great river at points where the gates of the rich landowners are ajar. Wealthy, religious, or nonprofit organizations such as the Marydell Convent and Fellowship of Reconciliation (FOR) also occupy waterfront estates along Broadway. I am not aware of any estate owners who provide for public access to the river.

The large riverfront mansion owned by the FOR, a public-spirited group whose aim it is to bring the peoples of the world closer together, usually appears deserted. A group of Shorewalkers who visited the FOR mansion bought a few pamphlets and buttons, and were welcomed by several FORers. FOR could strike a blow for openness by inviting the public to use their property to reach the river.

The only bus stop in town is across from the ornate Upper Nyack Town Hall and fire station on Broadway. From here one can catch the Red and Tan bus to the PATH terminals at 42nd Street or at 178th Street in New York City, a pleasant ride of about half an hour. The deli at this intersection has good sandwiches and a respectable selection of beers. One can sit at the table outdoors or on the steps and greet friendly dogs as they amble by. No public urinals are in evidence; however, there are secluded places nearby where one can relieve oneself. At the north end of Broadway in Upper Nyack the roadway bifurcates. Our path goes northeast along the river, but an alternate route over Hook Mountain may appeal to hardier hikers.

The trek over the rim of the mountain can be arduous, especially in warm weather. Bring at least a quart of water. To find the path, walk north on Midland Avenue, which parallels Broadway 1 block to the west. At the end of Midland a signed trailhead leads to a blazed trail, part of the Long Path. This trail quickly climbs first the south side and then the west side of stately Hook Mountain. At 729 feet high, Hook is the second tallest peak of the Palisades. The trail then crosses the hills called the Seven Sisters. When the trees are bare, one can glimpse panoramic views of the surrounding mountainous and watery regions. This rocky crest commands spectacular vistas of Rockland and Congers lakes to the west, beyond which are the

Ramapos. To the north rise the Hudson Highlands, Dunderberg, and the Timp. Northeast of the river rises rugged Breakneck Ridge. To the east lies Westchester County; to the south see the panorama of the wide Hudson crossed by the Tappan Zee Bridge and the Piermont mile-long pier jutting into the river. Farther south rise the cliffs of Tallman Mountain.

The cliff-top trail continues over a narrow, sinuous ridge with trees on either side. From occasional openings on the hilltops one glimpses Rockland Lake—once a major source of ice for New York City. One follows the turquoise markers on the south side of the rocks—note on the south side of outcrops the New York State prickly pear cactus, which bears bright yellow flowers. It should take about four hours to trek from the Hook across the Seven Sisters, a distance of a little more than 3 miles. Continue for another 3 miles over less-difficult terrain down to the lower ground on the shore.

So much for the high road. Let us now take the Batt to Bear low road.

▼ *Nyack Beach State Park*

Wikimedia Commons/Dmadeo

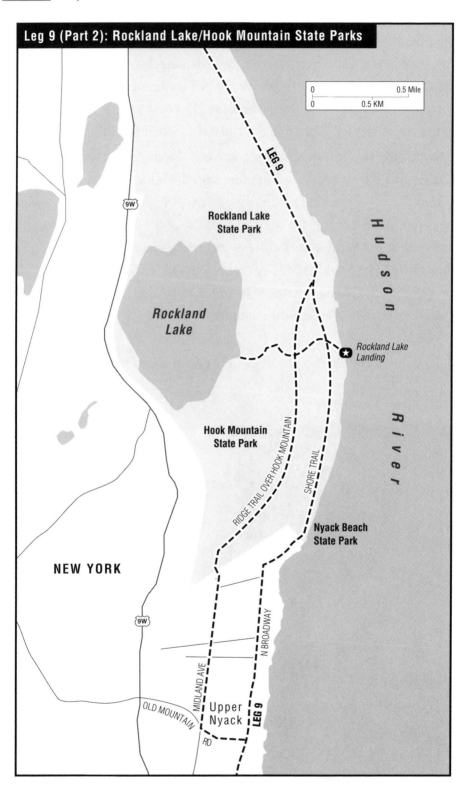

Leg 9 (Part 2): Rockland Lake/Hook Mountain State Parks

0   0.5 Mile
0   0.5 KM

LEG 9

Rockland Lake
State Park

Hudson

Rockland
Lake

Rockland Lake
Landing

Hook Mountain
State Park

River

RIDGE TRAIL OVER HOOK MOUNTAIN

SHORE TRAIL

Nyack Beach
State Park

NEW YORK

9W

N BROADWAY

MIDLAND AVE

OLD MOUNTAIN

Upper
Nyack

LEG 9

RD

Hook Mountain State Park, east of Rockland Lake State Park (845-268-3020; www.nysparks.state.ny.us), is a green, 676-acre rocky peninsula that bulges into the Hudson between Nyack and Haverstraw. The park abuts Nyack Beach State Park (845-268-3020; www.nysparks.state.ny.us) to the south, where one can bathe, fish, and bike along a shore trail.

In 1872 a large stone crusher was set up on Hook Mountain to break up Palisades rock and bring stone building materials to the growing cities along the Hudson. By the 1920s all quarries had ceased operation, and a shore path was built below the mountain. Most of Hook Mountain State Park is still rugged and undeveloped.

Just beyond the last large shore house in Upper Nyack abutting the park, about 200 feet from the park entrance, is a wooded area and a cluster of trees. Climb down a narrow flight of stone steps and descend through the woods to Nyack Beach State Park. This short, unmarked trail is easy to follow for a few hundred yards to the first picnic grounds of the park. At the water's edge are parking facilities, waterside picnic tables, drinking water, and toilets. The beach at the south end is becoming increasingly popular as the Hudson gets cleaner.

Initially the path going north is relatively flat, 6 to 10 feet above the water level, with striking views of the river; of Ossining, with famous Sing Sing Prison; of the green banks of the Hudson; and of other smaller east shore Hudson towns. Along this curving southern part of the shore trail, the vines, flowers, and leaves wave along the path in spring; in summer the leafy trees protect the walker from the sun. In fall the ground is strewn with golden, red, yellow, and brown leaves that sparkle in the sunlight.

Walker, beware the twilight hereabouts in the lee of Hook Mountain, where darkness can descend like a third-act curtain. One summer evening in 1990, twilight caught me on the path. Darkness dropped over the path about 7 PM as I was halfway to Haverstraw. Fortunately, the ground was dry. For 2 miles I picked my way with a stick along the blackened, winding trail, hoping to spy a light or some sign of friendly life. Feeling one's way along a pitch black, rocky path with a stick is not the most comfortable way to walk this trail. One becomes acutely aware of strange sounds: waves lapping on the rocks to the east, wild animals, the crunch of leaves on the ground, the wind in the trees, rustling leaves, a railroad freight train somewhere in the northern part of the park . . . I reached the outskirts of Haverstraw in one shaken piece.

The northern part of the Hook Mountain shore path starts where the road from Rockland Lake descends to the Hudson. We see a delightful picnic area with benches along the shore. North of this landing the path becomes much hillier and serpentine than the southern section. We spot the remains of an old railroad trestle, which jut out in spots not covered by trees and vines. Now the Conrail single-track freight line runs to the west of the Batt to Bear Trail mainly through a tunnel under the northern end of the park.

The river comes close to the steep slopes far below the path. Impressive sheer cliffs loom to the west. Near the end of the park path is a plaque marking the spot where general-turned-traitor Benedict Arnold met with British captain Andre.

The path emerges from deep woods into Dutchtown, a small riverside community of 50 or so houses stretched along Riverside Avenue.

▲ *The north end of the trail leads to Dutchtown and Haverstraw.*

▲ *Sculptor Theodore Ludwiczak's home features displays of his work.*

When school is out on a warm day, a few children and dogs roam the main street. One can sometimes find the elderly sculptor Theodore Ludwiczak of 14 Riverside Avenue, chisel in hand, displaying his stone heads, which are vaguely reminiscent of those of Easter Island. Dozens of his stone and wooden carvings decorate his modest housefront and lawn.

Riverside Avenue leads to the Tilcon Properties, an immense stone, sand, and gravel complex, with massive concrete silos and 30-foot-high piles of gravel. I find this an exciting visual contrast to the green jumble of bushes and trees in Hook Mountain State Park. Along the dusty road squat several large, dormant quarries, and the Tilcon Company's monumental facilities for moving sand, concrete, and gravel onto Hudson River barges moored in the bay at the company piers. Enormous overhead conveyers, sinuous piping, and majestic silos—a delight to my eye—dominate the skyline.

In the 1980s nothing grew here, but in 1990 Tilcon seeded the sloping area leading to the road, and trees were planted on Tilcon property along

Peter Nekola

▲ *Coming into Haverstraw, with High Tor in the distance*

the road to Haverstraw. By 1995 many evergreen trees had taken root and thrived, giving a greener, more pleasant aspect to the otherwise barren road. By 2011 the Tilcon road was lush with trees and shrubbery.

Directly north of Tilcon, the Harbors at Haverstraw, a large upscale housing development of about 200 condos and townhouses, was constructed in the 1990s. It is a different community from most of old Haverstraw. There are plans, in abeyance, to enlarge it to 800 units. Many of the Harbors' residents commute to work in Westchester County and New York City by taking the ferry, which docks nearby. The ferry crosses Haverstraw Bay mainly during commuter hours to Ossining, where one can catch a Metro-North train to New York City.

Follow Riverside Avenue into Haverstraw for half a mile, where the road changes its name to Broadway. This leads through an undistinguished neighborhood of one- and two-family houses. I prefer veering east from Broadway to the more scenic Hudson shore. Walk along First Street,

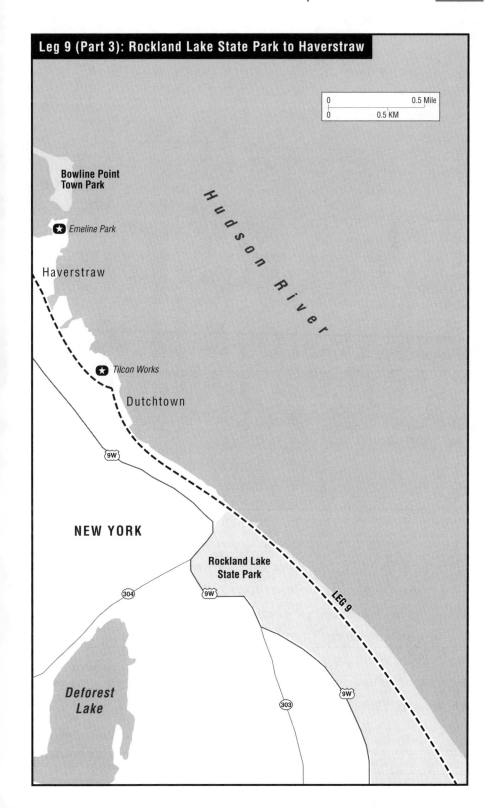

Leg 9 (Part 3): Rockland Lake State Park to Haverstraw

0   0.5 Mile
0   0.5 KM

H u d s o n   R i v e r

Bowline Point Town Park

★ *Emeline Park*

Haverstraw

★ *Tilcon Works*

Dutchtown

9W

NEW YORK

Rockland Lake State Park

LEG 9

304

9W

Deforest Lake

303

9W

▲ *A Haverstraw waterfront mansion; reminder of faded glory days.*

where several substantial 19th-century brick mansions bear witness to the former wealth Haverstraw enjoyed when it was a center of brickmaking. A changed economy and automotive throughways killed much of the local industry. A plaque along the shore commemorates the disastrous landslide of 1906 that killed 19 people. That slide was caused by excessive removal of clay from the Hudson River banks for making bricks.

A palatial brick mansion set in a big field on the cliff above Haverstraw Bay, now the Elks's headquarters, sits above Vincent's Landing. Nearby on a post on First Street is a plaque marking The widest part of the Hudson—about 4 miles across.

The town of Haverstraw sits in a cove on Haverstraw Bay, across from Tarrytown. Its attractions include riverside Emeline and Bowline parks, beautiful views of the river to the east and of the Palisades to the west, and friendly people.

▲ *The widest part of the Hudson.*

Pete Nekola

Emeline Park, a small playground and picnic ground at the foot of Main Street on the Hudson, is named after a side-wheeler ferry that graced the area in the 1890s and early part of the 20th century when the town was relatively wealthy. A rich industrialist bought the ferry in 1883 and named it after his mother. Before that it had been used by General Grant in the Civil War. The Scenic Hudson Land Trust acquired a significant portion of the Hudson shore known as Vincent's Landing in the 1990s, which doubled the size of Emeline Park. The waterfront now has a walking trail.

▼ *Kids were fishing in Haverstraw Bay when we passed by in 2011.*

▲ *View of the village of Haverstraw from atop*   Wikimedia Commons/Thomas McGuire
High Tor Mountain. Power plant is on the left.

In the 1950s Puerto Ricans settled in Haverstraw, drawn by jobs in the area and low-cost housing—mostly brick two-story structures left by the former brickyard workers. In recent years Dominicans arrived. Bodegas, mimosa trees, the bay, and Spanish music help give the Village of Haverstraw east of Broadway the feel of a Caribbean island. I estimate more than half of Haverstraw's residents are Latinos.

The village had extensive gravel and gypsum industries, several marinas, and the massive Bowline power plant, all of which squat in monumental proportions along its meandering riverbanks. West of the town rise the vertical cliffs of the Palisades. High Tor, an 827-foot peak of the Verdrietig Range overshadowing the town, is well worth a climb along the clearly marked trail.

A bit of history: "The glimpse from a passing steamer or railway train is all that the casual traveler will care to see of Haverstraw, which is a village that has grown up behind some 2 miles of brickyards, where hundreds of men are mining and molding and baking the fine clay sediment that settled in the eddies of that nook in the by-gone time when the stream was wider and deeper than now. They even build coffer dams out into the river to rescue from its bed the valuable brick clay, and far more than half of all the brick made along the whole course of the river comes from these yards which reach to Grassy Point, the steamboat landing." Thus wrote Ernest Ingersoll in 1910.

Although brickmaking started in Haverstraw in 1815, no bricks are made here now. In 1883, 42 active brickyards lined the Hudson shore, and 300 million bricks per year were being shipped up and down the river. For a hundred years Haverstraw supplied New York City with 90 percent of its bricks for its building industry. Brickmaking stopped about 1925. The Haverstraw Brick Museum, at 12 Main Street (845-947-3505; www.haverstrawbrickmuseum .org), is worth a visit.

On Haverstraw's shore, Benedict Arnold met secretly with British spy Maj. John Andre on September 21, 1780, to plot the surrender of West Point. A boulder at the Hudson's edge, south of town, marks the Treason Site. Major Andre was captured in Tarrytown across the Hudson. He was tried and hanged at Old Tappan near Piermont on October 2, 1780. His prison cell can be viewed in the stone restaurant in Old Tappan.

In the early 1900s the riverfront neighborhood along First Street and Allison Avenue was the showplace of this thriving village. Grand Victorian mansions lined the cliffs overlooking Haverstraw Bay. One can still see several dozen of these imposing structures along the shore. The King's Daughters Library, built around 1903, is well worth a visit. Located at 85 Main Street at the corner of First Street, this landmarked, two-story building displays both classical and Renaissance revival styles. One can see finely detailed cornices, rusticated masonry, a wide frieze made of

▲ *Hudson River and West Point views, ca. 1860s*

Indiana limestone, and a handsome curved entrance bay. We found the atmosphere pleasant and the librarians charming and helpful.

The walk through the rest of Haverstraw affords the observant walker views of village architecture, which varies from Colonial, Greek revival, and Victorian to modern schlock and rectangular "mail order" ticky-tacky little houses. There is no fancy downtown area, but many well-kept houses line outlying streets, such as Walnut and Hudson, parallel to the river and the railroad tracks. At Main and Hudson, a large, well-maintained redbrick Presbyterian church dominates an area of substantial houses on tree-lined streets. The first church building went up in 1790. The present structure, with its cloister arches, was built in 1909. Maple Street, on the other hand, seems to have been cobbled together to provide inexpensive, low-rise row housing.

George M. Cohan, famed composer of "Yankee Doodle Dandy" and many other American standards, made his show business debut at the Broadway Theater in Haverstraw on July 4, 1887. Only a grimy metal plaque and an empty lot now mark the spot. Central Haverstraw along Broadway may lack grace, but it displays vitality. Tawdry two-story brick buildings, many in need of paint, line the street. A bright spot along Broadway is the Latin Star, where we have eaten more than a dozen times.

A favorite choice is an ample dish of rice and squid served in a large aluminum pot, paella style. Their salads, ceviche, flan, and mango *batidoes* are delicious and refreshing. Service is adequate and pleasant.

Union and Bar Latino are two of the better restaurants that have grown up since the year 2000 on Main Street. Somewhat fancier is Civile's at Vincent's Landing (845-429-3891; www.civiles.net), a restaurant located in a large stone mansion on the river's shore. It can be reached by a narrow cobblestone road at the end of Main Street, or by tying your yacht up to Civile's private dock. I suggest you call first.

The Adler Tavern/Mad House, which opened in 1880, was one of the few remaining watering holes in downtown Haverstraw that was not Latino-owned. It had the remains of a fancy marble and wood bar. On one visit, while we were standing at the bar (since there were no barstools), the brawny bartender told us that Latinos started coming to Haverstraw in the 1960s because of available jobs in the area and inexpensive houses east of Broadway. In 1994, the Adler Tavern changed management and was renamed the Mad House. On a hot summer Sunday afternoon on one of our visits, half a dozen men and women sat quietly drinking, while two men played pool in the rear and a Rowe-AMI jukebox played a popular ballad. A sandy-haired house painter drinking beer, who described himself as a "redneck," told us he had painted the tavern and restored some of the woodwork.

▼ *Broadway*   Peter Nekola

The economic decline of Haverstraw can be traced to a number of factors. A big cave-in along Haverstraw's shore in the 1940s that killed a great number of people; the decline of brickmaking; the building of the New York State Thruway, which bypassed Haverstraw; and the stopping of rail commuter service all contributed.

This old town sitting between the Palisades and the Hudson River is still vibrant: Few townsites in the lower Hudson area are so prettily situated. Spend a pleasant few hours wandering around the waterfront and slaking your thirst before heading for Bear Mountain.

Few travelers appear to find a reason to stop overnight in Haverstraw. Looking for a hotel at 9 PM on a Saturday proved to be a futile effort. On one visit, the phone book listed only one hotel, housed in a seedy-looking frame building on Main Street that caters to weekly paying clients. A big, pink-faced policeman on Broadway said to me, "You don't want to sleep in this town." Noisy, though peaceful, Spanish-speaking youngsters roamed the main downtown streets. Some walked hand in hand, reminding me of a peaceful Caribbean village. Weary, I took the cop's advice and spent the night at the Stony Point Motel on US 9W, a short taxi ride north of Haverstraw.

In town, I recommend the Bricktown Inn (845-429-8447; www.brick towninnbnb.com), at 112 Hudson Street. It is a charming bed & breakfast operated by hosts Michelle and Joe Natale.

To get to the town and bypass the journey, one can catch a Short Line bus from the PATH terminal at 42nd Street to West Haverstraw (junction US 9W and US 202). Local Rockland buses stop on Broadway.

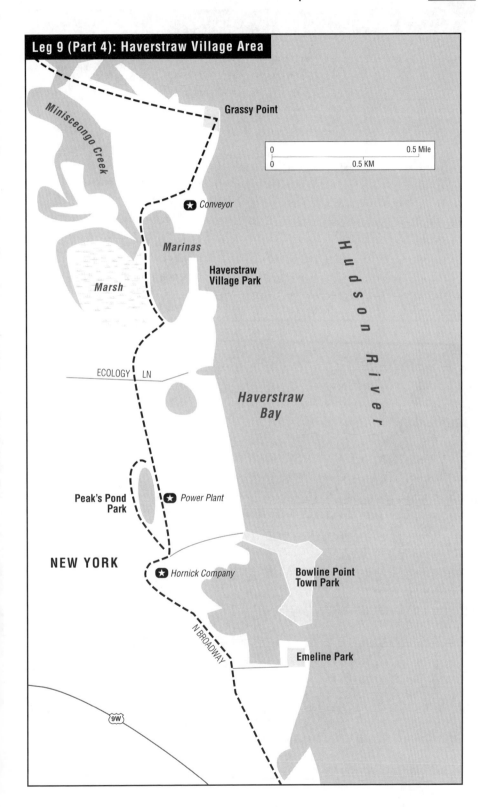

Leg 9 (Part 4): Haverstraw Village Area

Miniseongo Creek

Grassy Point

0   0.5 Mile
0   0.5 KM

⭐ Conveyor

Marinas

Haverstraw
Village Park

Marsh

Hudson River

ECOLOGY LN

Haverstraw
Bay

Peak's Pond
Park

⭐ Power Plant

NEW YORK

⭐ Hornick Company

Bowline Point
Town Park

N BROADWAY

Emeline Park

9W

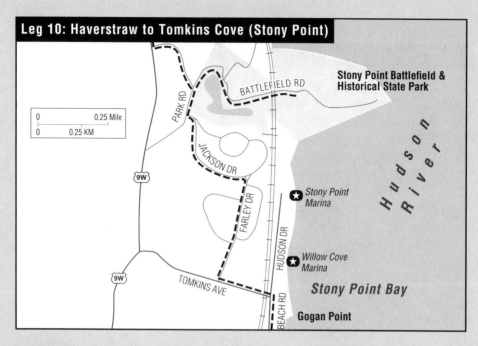

Leg 10: Haverstraw to Tomkins Cove (Stony Point)

0   0.25 Mile
0   0.25 KM

PARK RD

BATTLEFIELD RD

**Stony Point Battlefield &
Historical State Park**

JACKSON DR

9W

FARLEY DR

HUDSON DR

★ *Stony Point
Marina*

★ *Willow Cove
Marina*

9W

TOMKINS AVE

BEACH RD

Stony Point Bay

Gogan Point

*H u d s o n
R i v e r*

Peter Nekola

▲ *A park in Haverstraw*

LEG 10 | HAVERSTRAW TO TOMKINS COVE

ABOUT 5 TO 6 MILES THROUGH A MIXED URBAN, INDUSTRIAL, AND MARINE ENVIRONMENT

A mellow sunset was settling upon the hills and waters and a thousand flashes played over the distant city as its spires and prominent objects caught its glow.

—N. P. Willis

From Haverstraw to Bear Mountain, the Hudson shorewalker encounters a rugged, hilly coast, mostly still wooded, and green in the summer. We walk through the gorge in the Hudson Highlands. Here the Hudson was once lined with industrial complexes—monuments to human industry and power. Isolated villages, ramshackle river houses, and stately mansions now add a unique accent to the natural display. Along this section of the Hudson River Shore Trail, the walker passes varied and exhilarating views of one of America's most beautiful and productive river valleys.

Leaving central Haverstraw, walk north along Broadway. We have two possible routes to the north: (1) along US 9W or (2) the meandering shore path, our recommended route.

This shore route takes a path that winds through Haverstraw along streets and through parks closer to

129

the Hudson. Start by walking north on Broadway past St. Peter's Roman Catholic Church (115 Broadway), an imposing redbrick building, the tallest in town except for the Bowline power plant. It is cool and quiet inside.

Peter Nekola

▲ *Ecology Lane, Haverstraw*

Broadway in Haverstraw follows relatively high ground above the river and affords expansive views of the bay and across to the Westchester shore. We walk about half mile north of the church, passing a neatly clipped block-long lawn in front of a modern industrial building. This belongs to the Hornick Company. On the lawn are examples of monumental modern sculpture, contrasting sharply with the rather seedy, two-story buildings that line the west side of Broadway. Walk to a wide street, Samsondale, which leads east to pretty Bowline Point Park and to the massive cubic structures and smokestack of the Bowline power plant. Bowline Point Park juts out into the river on a small peninsula and is much used by local residents for fishing, swimming, and picnicking.

Back on our route and the unsigned road, turn left on a road that leads between the Bowline power plant and Peak's Pond Park. An asphalt road surrounds Peak's Pond and is lined with imposing trees. We pass a new shed with plantings around it, and then a Little League playing field—Babe Ruth Field—and walk around one side of the pond for several hundred yards to County Route 108 (Railroad Avenue). Once past Peak's Pond, continue north along the road, which winds parallel to Minisceongo Creek for approximately a quarter mile to Beach Road.

Follow this quiet, curving road north between reed meadows, car lots, marshes, and the city dump (or "recycling plant"). No beach is in evidence, but Minisceongo Creek bubbles merrily to the east, running amid trees and shrubs. A few ducks paddle about in a shady summer pool. Cross Ecology Lane and pass a tool works on the west. After about a 15-minute walk of less than a mile we come upon several large marinas. Large yachts and expensive boats bob in the water. Minisceongo Creek and marshy lands lie to the west.

Continue walking north along Beach Road, which changes its name to Hudson Drive, Grassy Point Road, and then River Road as we enter Stony Point. Few vehicles drive along it.

Come to a tubular overhead viaduct conveyor that arches over the shore road and the marina to a dock in the river. The landward end of the conveyor sits among large mounds of brownish rock behind a high metal-wire fence.

The mounded material, we subsequently discovered, was gypsum. These pyramids of pink added variety to the landscape. Gypsum, or hydrous calcium sulfate, is fabricated into plaster of Paris and wallboard. As of August 2011, the plant seems to no longer be in operation. Danny Sheeran, of Sheeran's excellent restaurant and pub (337 North Liberty Drive, Tomkins Cove; 845-429-6190), told us that the gypsum plant left because of high taxes. He said that the closing of this plant, and of the coal-burning power plant, and of Tilcon, had greatly diminished the taxable income to the Tomkins Cove area, and that as a result, the homeowners were paying much higher real estate taxes to make up the shortfall.

▲ *Sheeran's Restaurant and Pub*

The striking gypsum industrial complex stands in sharp contrast to the fancy pleasure boats bobbing nearby in Haverstraw Bay, and to the wilderness on High Tor above Haverstraw. A road worker, shovel in hand, said: "Most of these fancy boats belong to rich people from New Jersey. Around here we local river people have to work for a living."

Continue strolling with the river to the east. About a mile north at Grassy Point, the road veers sharply to the west, closely following the shore. Rockland County has opened a park where the road bends. Though it is marked for residents only, the attendant allowed hikers to use the toilets and drink Rockland water from park fountains. We assured the attendant that our use of park toilets would only recycle beer and sodas bought in Rockland County. One warm September Sunday, we saw kids swimming here, a young mother sitting on the riverbank under a tulip tree suckling her infant, sailboats drifting in the bay. Simple wood frame houses overlook the wide bay.

That same day, with the noonday sun beating down from a clear sky, three of us stopped at the Deck Bar, the only

▶ *The Minisceongo Creek shipwreck*

watering place open along this stretch of the shore. We were warmly greeted with air-conditioning and cold drinks. Locals bellying up to the bar eyed we shorewalkers curiously: "Lose your license? Did they steal your car?" We assured them we were walking along the river because we enjoyed it. Alas, this friendly and pleasant spot closed in 1992. Do not despair; beer is up ahead at Gilligan's on the Hudson (845-942-3966), at 10 Grassy Point Road in Stony Point. It has a wonderful view.

About a quarter mile farther north of the park along the pleasant shore road, cross the mouth of winding Minisceongo Creek, which here widens into a lake. In the shallows sits an old shipwreck of what appears to have been a large barge. Inch-thick iron rivets and nails stick up through a wooden framework blackened by fire.

The ship's structure rivals, in design and execution, many modern art sculptures I have seen. This exposed industrial monument is the handiwork

▲ *Entrance to Stony Point Battlefield State Historic Site*

of American craftsmen, engineers, and boatbuilders, modified by changing economic needs; Mother Nature, the creative destroyer; and ravaging time.

Continue walking along Stony Point Bay, cross a small bridge over the mouth of Minisceongo Creek, and cut to the right, east along a road called Hudson Drive and/or Beach Road in Stony Point, a community of about 12,000 residents. Along the curving shore few humans are in evidence.

To our west runs the raised railroad bed; to our east flows the Hudson. Boatyards line Stony Point Bay. After several hundred yards, walk under the raised Conrail railroad track onto Tomkins Avenue. A bicycle trail runs through the neighborhood, traveling from the marina district and passing the battlefield's entrance drive, where Park Road intersects with Battlefield Road. Battlefield Road leads east into the Stony Point Battlefield State Historic Site. The shade trees are most welcome in sunny, warm weather.

Stony Point peninsula juts into the Hudson on high ground. This rocky ledge was the site of a major battle during the Revolutionary War. The British took the point on May 29, 1779, to control the King's Ferry, a key Hudson River transportation link used by the Colonial army. On the night of July 15, 1779, Gen. "Mad Anthony" Wayne led his Pennsylvania light infantry corps in a surprise bayonet assault that took the British fort. The battle ended British activity in the north and along the Hudson. It was one of the few Colonial victories along the Hudson. A museum, picnic pavilion, lighthouse, and vantage points dot this rocky and impressive site.

On earlier scouting expeditions I have climbed the high hill on Stony Point peninsula to the lookout for King's Ferry. A sweeping panorama of the river and its green shores comes into view. I also heard and saw a 100-car train of coal gondolas, like a caravan of massive black-humped camels, moving slowly north to a power plant, which was demolished in 2008. Now only a bare, closed-off area along the river marks the spot where it stood.

Exiting Stony Point, walk west on Battlefield Road to US 9W, and then walk north on 9W for about 2 miles, through the community of Tomkins Cove.

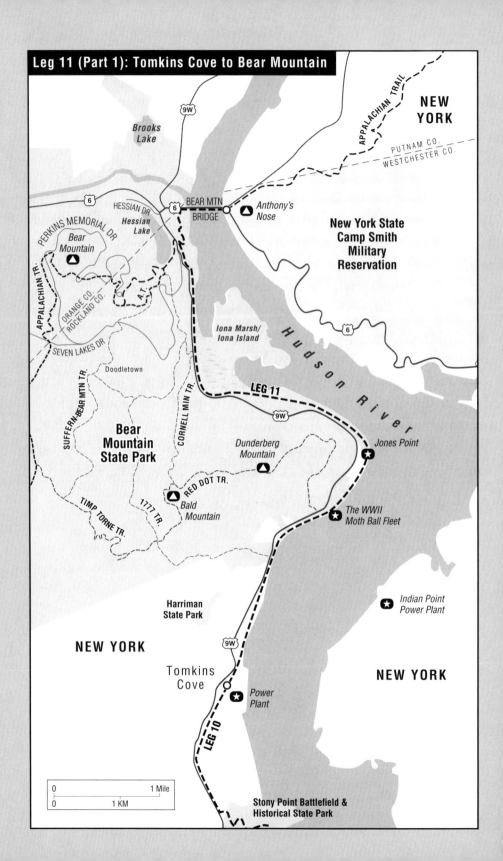

Leg 11 (Part 1): Tomkins Cove to Bear Mountain

9W

Brooks Lake

NEW YORK

APPALACHIAN TRAIL

PUTNAM CO.
WESTCHESTER CO.

6

HESSIAN DR

BEAR MTN BRIDGE

PERKINS MEMORIAL DR

Hessian Lake

6

Anthony's Nose

Bear Mountain

New York State
Camp Smith
Military
Reservation

APPALACHIAN TR.

ORANGE CO.
ROCKLAND CO.

A.T.

SEVEN LAKES DR

*Iona Marsh/
Iona Island*

Hudson River

SUFFERN-BEAR MTN TR.

Doodletown

CORNELL MTN. TR.

LEG 11

6

Bear Mountain State Park

Dunderberg Mountain

9W

Jones Point

TIMP TORNE TR.

1777 TR.

RED DOT TR.

Bald Mountain

The WWII
Moth Ball Fleet

Harriman State Park

Indian Point
Power Plant

NEW YORK

9W

Tomkins
Cove

NEW YORK

Power
Plant

LEG 10

0 ——————— 1 Mile
0 ——————— 1 KM

**Stony Point Battlefield &
Historical State Park**

LEG 11 | TOMKINS COVE TO BEAR MOUNTAIN

ABOUT 5 TO 6 MILES MAINLY OVER HILLY FOREST PATHS

On his view

Ocean and earth, and

heaven burst before him,

Clouds slumbering at his

feet and the clear blue

Of summer's sky in beauty

bending o'er him.

—Fitz-Greene Halleck

Walk north from Stony Point. Tilcon Corporation once operated a large quarry here, directly south of the demolished Orange & Rockland coal-fired power plant. It was sobering to watch a string of 100 coal gondolas being unloaded, to observe huge mounds of stored coal in the wintertime, and to see the tall chimneys looming over the plant's vast coal storage and handling facilities. America is well endowed with coal. Burning the black fossil rocks is still the major way Americans generate the magic electrical energy without which our sprawling suburbs and great cities could not exist.

The old Orange & Rockland plant was "private property" indeed. A guardhouse on the road

◀ *The Tilcon quarry was virtually abandoned by 2011*

leading to the south end of the plant stopped all cars and discouraged road walkers. However, if one happened to be walking along (but not on) the rail tracks, as we did on several occasions in the 1985–1995 era, one was simply exercising the right of innocent passage, in my opinion. Now, in 2012, it is not possible to walk through; a locked gate blocks passage. The current owner, Consolidated Edison, does not permit it.

▲ *The Orange & Rockland power plant stood here years earlier. The land is now owned by Con Edison. (Note the single track, used by Conrail to bring stuff to Jersey City and the metropolitan NYC area.)*

Now, one must skirt the massive Orange & Rockland power plant property by climbing a curving, paved road past Hansen Place. Here one finds "Pa's Place" and "Mom's Street," a small triangular playground set in a sharp curve of the road (Spring Street) decorated with sculptures welded from large gears, pistons, and other components from old industrial plants. We proceed along a narrow access road leading north. Climb past several single-family houses along shady Spring Street and then exit through two massive stone stanchions left over from a now-demolished mansion.

Passing through these stanchions, we came upon the three-story Boulderberg Manor, built like a Swiss chalet, a remnant of a bygone age. In the early 1990s it was in use as a fancy restaurant, but it is no longer. This unique building was erected by industrialist Calvin Tomkins around the time of the Civil War. It was designed by Andrew Jackson Downing in Hudson River Gothic style and was the first poured concrete building in New York State. Lacy plaster moldings, fine woodwork, plush appointments, old pictures, and an intimate bar attest to Tomkins's tastes and wealth. Cold beer was available when the chateau was open in 1991. More recently, we found it had been bought and turned into a private dwelling.

The manor, built on a promontory overlooking the Hudson River, affords magnificent views once marred by the Orange & Rockland plant below it on the shore of the Hudson.

In 1990, on the north side of the Boulderberg property we spotted an overgrown path leading northeasterly down the slope toward the river. We followed this path through the brush. We decided to scout it rather than go along US 9W or the railroad track, as we had on other occasions. The overgrown path leads north beneath a row of giant 50-foot-high concrete pylons that support electric power lines running from the power plant. The pylons look like giant white trees with stubby branches trunks holding the wires. Colorful and varied wildflowers abound in June. Weeds and brambles line the way until the path peters out. We continued through the brush for about 10 minutes downhill as the path wound toward the river, bushwhacking part of the way through the trees, then walked down to the railroad right-of-way. After walking parallel to the tracks for about five minutes, we switched to Gays Hill Road, which runs less than 10 yards from, and parallel to, the track.

With the river to the east, follow quiet Gays Hill Road through Tomkins Cove between Buckberg Mountain and the Hudson. This pleasant, little-used secondary road is much preferable to busy 9W. A handful of neat frame houses line the road. Few cars come by. Because of a jurisdictional dispute in 1995, Gays Hill Road had its name changed to West Shore Drive. Alas.

An alternate route north from Boulderberg is along US 9W, which climbs steeply in this area. Bicyclists use this road, along with fast moving trucks and cars. One pleasant feature of this route is the tavern on top of a rise in the road, where one can sip a beer while looking out over the Hudson.

From the hilltop, 9W dips down and runs parallel to, and a few yards from, the railroad track. A plaque along the road commemorates the Hudson River Defense Reserve Fleet, which was moored here for several years after 1946. At its peak, the "mothball fleet" consisted of 189 World War II Liberty Ships. The ships were used as floating grain silos for a time. They "served our country well," according to the U.S. Department of Commerce Maritime Administration, which put up the plaque in 1971. Most of the ships were sold to Greek and other foreign owners, enterprising shippers who made fortunes running the old ships during the booming 1950s and 1960s.

Here, one can easily cross the Conrail tracks to the Hudson beach where local residents troll for striped bass. This is a pleasant place to stop, to gaze over the water, take a sip, and have lunch.

Across the Hudson under two thick concrete domes loom two Indian Point nuclear reactors. In 2011, Con Edison drew more than 30 percent of its electric energy from the Indian Point power plant. The plant emits no noxious hydrocarbons or oxides and does not add to the greenhouse effect. The reactors may someday malfunction, leak, or even explode.

▼ *Examining the plaque commemorating the Hudson River Defense Reserve Fleet, 2011.*

▲ *Indian Point supplied Con Edison with more than 30 percent of its electric power in 2011.*

This probability, is, I believe, as likely as being struck dead by a falling watermelon. You and I have a much better chance dying in an automobile accident. River water flowing both ways past the domes is used as a coolant. The reactors supply Con Edison with relatively low-cost electricity.

Before the 1950s, Con Edison generated most of its electricity from coal, which, when burnt, gives off black soot, smoke, and sulphur dioxide. In 2011, Con Edison said that it got 60 percent of its fuel from gas, 35 percent from nuclear power, and only 5 percent from coal-fired generators.

North of Tomkins Cove, US 9W runs parallel and close to the Conrail freight tracks, separated only by a wide shoulder. After a 20-minute stroll, we arrive at a fork in the road with signs saying DEAD END and, to the right, JONES POINT. This small community was renamed for one Charles H. Jones. This isolated riverside bulge used to be called Kidd's Point in honor of Captain Kidd, the pirate. Kidd was reputed to have buried a large Spanish treasure hereabouts; to my knowledge, no Spanish gold has ever been found. Old maps show the "Kidd Point" designation.

Just south of Jones Point stands a stately old stone church abutting a wide, green field. One hot Sunday we came upon a nonalcoholic frolic of not-so-anonymous Rockland County AAs and their friends. Hundreds of

▲ *A wide road along the track parallels 9W. Pete Nekola and Ed Liebowitz enjoying the sun.*

men, women, and children were broiling hamburgers, smoking cigarettes, and drinking soda pop. They invited us to join them, and we indulged in soda pop. But the sun was sinking, and we had to hurry if we were to reach Bear Mountain before dark and catch the last bus back to New York City.

Isolated Jones Point juts east into the river. Directly to its west rise Dunderberg and Bald mountains, both within Bear Mountain State Park. The Red Dot trail leads to Bald Mountain. One can follow this sinuous path to the Timp, then to the steep winding trails to Doodletown, and then to the Bear Mountain Bridge; it's a sinuous and strenuous path through the mountains

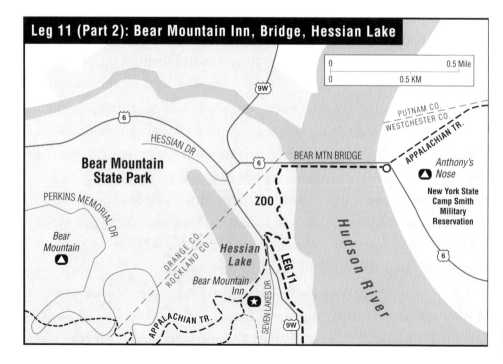

from north to south. To my mind the riverside path is more varied, scenic, and certainly less arduous. Walk through the only street of Jones Point, which, hugging the Hudson shore, consists of about 25 houses and leads to a dead end. The riverside Conrail freight tracks define the community's eastern edge. Residents cross the track to fish, swim, and boat. They walk along the tracks as a matter of course. Bear Mountain Park hems in the community from the west and north.

Dunderberg marks the southern gate of the Hudson Highlands. We now walk along a twisting section of river: the Hudson Highlands that stretch 15 miles along the Hudson River as it cuts through the Appalachian chain of mountains, an old mountain range stretching 2,000 miles from Maine to Georgia. The Appalachian Highlands rise up from the shore between Peekskill Bay and Newburgh Bay as the meandering Hudson flows fast and narrow, compared to the relatively flat and wide stretches to the north and south of the Highlands. Depths of 80- to 200-foot channels attest to the scouring force of swift Hudson Highland currents. On both sides of the Hudson, peaks of over 1,000 feet create beautiful, rugged, mysterious landscapes. The highest mountains rise straight up from the swift water: Storm King on the north, Dunderberg on the south, Breakneck, Anthony's

▲ *Stereoscopic card of the Hudson, near West Point, ca. 1870*   Wikimedia Commons/E. & H. T. Anthony (Firm)

Nose, Bear Mountain . . . Fortunately for today's nature lover, this rough terrain dissuaded early settlers and builders. Today the region is further protected by the extensive Palisades Interstate Park and the 16,000-acre U.S. military reservation at West Point, north of Bear Mountain.

In fall, riverside mountains blaze with red, orange, and yellow leaves; colors flow down the steep slopes into the blue waters there to reflect their vibrancy. Beauty abounds in all seasons—in winter, when lack of deciduous leaves gives the walker clearer views of the stone mountains and the water's edge; in summer, when nature is in full leaf and the shore dresses in shades of darker green; in springtime, delicate young leaves and plants push tentatively out of the sparse soil into the riverine environment.

Near a house on the north end of town is an unmarked little-used trailhead: a sign says BIKE ROUTE. Once part of old 9W, this narrow but easy-to-follow shaded dirt trail winds up through the park toward Bear Mountain.

▲ *You never know who—or what—you will meet on the path.*

In June 2011, we encountered here a 5-foot-long black rat snake sunbathing in our path. We shouted at it! It coiled to strike. We threw sticks at it until it finally decided to slither into the underbrush to let the four of us pass.

For about 3 miles we walk beneath the flank of Dunderberg Mountain through old woods, with the Hudson River to the east. Wild roses and honeysuckle bloom in June. Older maps refer to this trail as the "Jones Point Road." From the shady lane we spy majestic panoramas of the river:

the Bear Mountain Bridge, Iona Island, and Iona Marsh. A Conrail freight train barreling along the single track somewhere below whistles to us.

Productive Iona Marsh suckles fish, wildlife, various birds, and marine animals. Rocky Iona Island sits on a unique promontory once used by the U.S. government as a shipping and transport facility. All we observed on a 1995 visit was a couple with butterfly nets. On previous visits I met Boy Scouts camping here. The solid brick buildings appear to be unused. The large iron gate leading to Iona Island, east of the railroad tracks, is usually chained. A large hole in the fence 200 yards north of the gate entices the curious.

Droppings along the path indicate use by deer and other animals. I have rarely seen any humans on it. After about 4 miles, this delightful path runs into less-delightful 9W. The walker wishing to avoid 9W may cross the road to the wooded Doodletown path, which leads to the Bear Mountain Inn. Hikers in a hurry follow the shoulder of 9W for the next 1.3 miles. Refreshments, beer, food, toilets, and other amenities used to await the weary walker at this substantial stone and wood-paneled inn. Alas, the Bear Mountain Inn has been closed since 2005, ostensibly for "repairs."

▼ *The Hudson River, looking north from the Bear Mountain Bridge.*

Wikimedia Commons/Rolf Müller

To me, it is counterproductive to keep such a solid and potentially useful building from public use for so long. New York State is delinquent to allow this wonderful resource to languish. However, the Overlook Lodge at Bear Mountain Inn offers accommodations with kitchenettes.

Continue walking from the Bear Mountain Inn north along Hessian Lake, named for the 200 or so dead Hessian soldiers (Germans hired by the British during the American Revolution) tossed into it by Washington's troops. Come to, and follow, the Appalachian Trail, which here runs west to east. Along the trail from the inn to the bridge nestles the charming Bear Mountain Trailside Museum and Wildlife Center (845-786-2701; www. trailsidezoo.org). Here, native wild animals and several excellent ecological exhibits are well worth stopping for. Beautiful ospreys, two fat black bears, a coyote, red and white foxes, and eagles were there when we visited. Clean toilets add to the allure of the museum.

Follow the Appalachian Trail to the roundabout and over the Bear Mountain Bridge. This is probably the lowest elevation along the 2,000-mile Appalachian Trail. Breathtaking views of the winding river gorge and the Hudson Highlands from the center of this graceful suspension bridge alone are worth the trip. Gazing at the dark green highlands, the river, its wavy banks, the blue sky, and the bridge, we are reminded of the

▼ *View of the Bear Mountain Bridge over the Hudson River, 2009*

Shorewalker motto: "Collecting things is good; Shorewalking is better."

But we must go back to the big city. To return to the New York Metropolitan area from Bear Mountain Inn without a car, one may take the Short Line bus (800-631-8405; www.shortlinebus.com), which meanders along US 9W to Paramus, New Jersey, and then through the Lincoln Tunnel to the Port Authority terminal at West 42nd Street. In 2011, buses from Bear Mountain ran at 3:19 PM and 5:19 PM and cost $13.50 one-way. (Buses to Bear Mountain leave Port Authority at 8:45 AM and 11:45 AM.) On weekends one can usually catch one of the two Metro-North evening trains, which can be flagged down at the minute East Hudson community of Manitou. To get to Manitou, walk east from Bear Mountain Inn over the Bear Mountain Bridge. One used to be able to clamber down the sloping dirt path north of the bridge to the river's edge. In the 1990s, one could walk parallel beside the railroad tracks to Manitou, making certain to avoid the tracks: Fast-moving trains rush silently out of the tunnel. Now, in 2012, it is safer to walk east from the bridge than cut north and west to Manitou. If you miss the Manitou train, walk another 6 miles north on the access road parallel to the tracks to Garrison, a larger, more active railroad stop. You won't starve or go dry in Garrison.

All elements of life mingle while walking along the Hudson shore.

Wikimedia Commons/Ahodges7

CODA

We walk along an unknown shore to see what wonders are hidden around the next bend. And we walk to find ourselves. Ultimately, all long journeys are voyages toward home; some have traveled to Himalaya, Rome, Mecca, or Tsingfu searching for images of renewal. Seeking for the unknown, I prefer to walk along the Hudson, which touches nature and mankind; it is closer to home and less expensive.

Scouting the Hudson River Shore Trail, I have encountered great beauty, exotic cultures, wild animals, friendly companions, a sense of joy and accomplishment, frustrations, and spiritual delights. I hope to pass my findings on to others who explore and walk the waterfront.

▼ *Hudson River Greenway Trail parallels the Batt to Bear route in Rockland County, but not in New Jersey.*

Peter Nekola

The idea of creating a walking trail from the mouth of the Hudson at the Battery in Manhattan to the high source in the Adirondacks developed first in 1982. In September 1984, the *New York Times* published my Op-Ed "For Hudsonophiles, a Long, Long Trail" (see XIX), which outlined the plan and the quest. This long, long trail is not yet complete. Other walkers have and will continue to

16 - Sierra Atlantic Fall, 1988

A Greenway to Where?

by Cy Adler

The Hudson River Greenway Study Bill passed overwhelmingly in the New York Senate and Assembly in July. The bill calls for the creation of a Greenway Commission to be appointed by Governor Mario Cuomo which will oversee a study of open space resources in the counties bordering the Hudson from Westchester to the Troy Dam.

The bill promotes the quaint notion that the Hudson River stops flowing at the Bronx border south of Westchester, and that no Hudson Valley exists north of Troy. No provision is made for protecting and enhancing open land and parks and trails along the Hudson in the New York State's Bronx and Manhattan counties. We would like to assure Upstate legislators that the Hudson does indeed continue past Yonkers, washing the shores of New York City as the river flows to the sea.

No mention is made in the Greenway bill of the Hudson River Shore Trail bill which will be the spine and living backbone of any Hudson Greenway. The 330 mile HRST walking path starts in Battery Park, runs along the Manhattan shore and goes north to the source of the river in the Adirondacks.

One trusts the "Greenway" will be more than a means of assuring beautiful scenic vistas for present landowners along Mid-Hudson counties. We hope the governor will appoint knowledgeable and aware persons familar with the Hudson's history, parks and linear paths.

The Greenway concept has great potential. If properly implemented, a green path will protect the Hudson. It will link state parks, abandoned railroads, scenic roads, walkways, and coastal promenades in a Hudson River Shore Hiking Path and it will assure all citizens a healthful and spirit-lifting pathway to follow.

pull on their boots and explore segments of the shore.

As a result of my article and the prodding of other Shorewalkers, in 1988 Governor Mario Cuomo formed the Hudson River Valley Greenway Council, ostensibly to create a greenway along the Hudson. Initially, the upstate promoters of this greenway tried to ignore New York City, though the Hudson runs along Manhattan and the Bronx, two boroughs of the city. (See the appended article "A Greenway to Where?") After several years and the expenditure of more than $1 million, in April 1991 the council issued its report, in which it proposed that a continuous trail be built along the Hudson River from Albany to New York City. The work continues and has led to several pretty parks and greenways along the Hudson.

City dwellers (and suburbanites, too) need quiet places that they do not have to share with automobiles. While the automobile is surely an amazing gadget, it is after all an inefficient mechanical monster that fouls our environment with noise and noxious gasses, and kills about 40,000 Americans a year—more in the future. Rational people are demanding auto-free parks and pathways such as the Hudson River Shore Trail. Join those thinking and concerned citizens.

Rivers, the creations of a wayward nature, often cut through municipalities, thus creating discrepancies between natural geographic systems and political subdivisions. This often makes the preservation of river basins, linear parks, and rivers themselves difficult. As you walk along the Hudson River Shore Trail from the Battery to Bear Mountain, you will stumble on littoral areas preempted by power plants, gravel and trash transfer stations, and private estates where one cannot dip a toe into the flowing river. But most of the way along the Hudson River—we would estimate more than 90 percent—the flowing water is close to the trail.

Two of the clearings along the Batt to Bear Trail abut rich marshes, wetland preserves that support large marine life and flocks of waterfowl whose cries echo over the river. The Iona and Piermont marshes are superb bird-watching locales.

Instead of walking the entire length of the path, one may canoe or bike parts of it. The way to Bear Mountain, and farther to Mount Marcy, offer a variety of car-free delights. Cars are poor contraptions for experiencing nature directly.

One must leave the city occasionally and immerse oneself in nature to refresh the spirit. Frederick Law Olmsted (a 19th-century designer of Central, Prospect, Riverside, and many other parks) considered green spaces to be an absolute necessity for the survival of the modern city. To Olmsted the increasing interest in nature was "a self-preserving instinct of civilization." I agree, our human species cannot sustain its evolutionary growth without regular contact with the natural wilderness from which we evolved.

Because the city is the most reasonable ecological niche for humans in the 21st century, and because modern life revolves about urban cores, we cannot abandon them. Indeed, Americans must inevitably convert our energy wasting carborne, land-grubbing suburbs into compact, mass-transit cities in order to live more harmoniously with nature. (See my book *Ecological Fantasies: Death from Falling Watermelons*, published in 1973.)

Reader, pull on your shoes and walk along the Hudson River. Compared to "health clubs" and yoga lessons, shorewalking costs little while providing improved health and other pleasures. And if the reader has a few spare dollars to help preserve the environment by helping to link up the Hudson River Shore Trail, the concerned walker-reader may send a gift to: Shorewalkers Inc., Box 20748, Cathedral, NY 10025. Shorewalkers Inc. is a 501(c)(3) entity and a New York State chartered not-for-profit corporation. Walk, give, and sing.

As your eyes take in the sky over the water and your nose sniffs the fresh air, bear in mind our motto: "Collecting things is good; shorewalking is better." Come walk with us along the banks of the still-green queen of rivers.

References and Useful Information

Transportation

BUSES	
Rockland Coaches	www.coachusa.com/rockland
Offers services in Rockland County and northern New Jersey.	
Port Authority Bus Terminal	212-564-8484
Main Office	201-384-2400
New York City	212-279-6526
Red and Tan Tours	www.coachusa.com/redandtan
Bus lines to Rockland Lake, Nyack, Piermont, Fort Lee, and points in between. Approximately hourly service on weekends.	
Port Authority Bus Terminal	212-736-4700
Short Line Buses	www.coachusa.com/shortline
Buses depart from New York City to Bear Mountain, Tomkins Cove, Haverstraw, and West Haverstraw, about five per day.	
From the PATH terminal at 42nd Street to Haverstraw (junction US 9W and US 202), a bus departs daily at 8:45 AM and arrives at 10:01 AM, and a second bus departs daily at 11:15 AM and arrives at 12:31 PM. As of 2011, $11 one-way.	
New York City	212-736-4700
Ridgewood, NJ	201-444-7005
Newburgh, NY	914-561-0734

TRAINS ALONG THE HUDSON	
Metro-North	www.mta.info
Stops sporadically on weekends at Manitou, a whistle stop 1 mile north of the Bear Mountain Bridge. Pleasant and scenic water-level trip to Marble Hill (connecting to the Broadway Local IRT #1) or to Grand Central Station.	

Rockland County Transit Information	www.co.rockland.ny.us 845-364-3333
Travel within the county via bus and train, or travel from the county via bus, train, and ferry. Info line	

FERRIES	
New York Waterway	www. newyorkwaterway.com 800-53-FERRY
Ferries run from Ossining to Haverstraw, among other routes.	

Lodging

INNS	
Bear Mountain Inn 55 Hessian Drive, Bear Mountain	845-786-2731 www.visitbearmountain.com
While the Bear Mountain Inn is currently closed, open on the property is the **Overlook Lodge**, *which offers a variety of accommodations with kitchenettes. Great hiking trails are nearby. There's little else in this area.*	

Parks and Historic Sites

New York State Office of Parks, Recreation & Historic Preservation,
www.nysparks.state.ny.us/

Books about the Hudson Valley and the River

*In addition to the following titles, the Hudson River Valley Institute (***www. hudsonrivervalley.org/library/***) has collected a wealth of information about the Hudson River Valley region in a variety of different media.*

References (abbreviated)

- Adams, Arthur G. *The Hudson River Guide Book*. New York: Fordham University Press, 1996. Extraordinary and fulsome: a compendium of information on places and history along the Hudson, especially for car drivers.

- Adler, Cy A. *Ecological Fantasies: Death from Falling Watermelons*. New York: Green Eagle Press, 1973 (www.greeneagle.org). A defense of innovation, science, and rational approaches to environmental problems.
- Adler, Cy A. *Walking Manhattan's Rim: The Great Saunter*, New York: Green Eagle Press, 2003 (www.greeneagle.org).
- The American Geographical Society and New York–New Jersey Trail Conference. *New York Walk Book*. Garden City and New York: Doubleday/ Natural History Press, 1971.
- Binnewies, R.O. *Palisades: 100,000 Acres in 100 Years*. New York: Fordham University Press, 2001.
- Boyle, Robert. *The Hudson River*. New York: W.W. Norton, 1979. An excellent book dealing with environment, fishing, and river topics.
- Bruce, Wallace. *The Hudson*. 1882, revised 1907. Reprinted by *Walking News*, POB 352, New York, NY 10013. *"Among all the rivers of the world the Hudson is acknowledged queen, decked with romance, jewelled with poetry, clad with history, and crowned with beauty. More than this, the Hudson is a noble threshold to a great continent and New York Bay a fitting portal."*
- Carmer, Carl. *The Hudson*. New York: Rinehart, 1939; 1974 edition.
- Dubos, Rene. *A God Within*. New York: Charles Scribner's Sons, 1972.
- Dunwell, Frances F. *The Hudson River Highlands*. New York: Columbia University Press, 1991. A beautiful and informative work on the most majestic and sinuous section of the lower Hudson.
- Grim, E and Schreiber E. P. *Riverside Park*. New York: Columbia University Press, 2007. Beautiful pictures and information about this Hudson River park in Manhattan.
- Lossing, Benson. *The Hudson, from the Wilderness to the Sea*, Delmar, NY: Black Dome Press , 2000. Reproduction of the informative 1866 edition. In his foreword, Pete Seeger writes "Lucky are the persons who hold a copy of this book in their hands."
- Marshall, Bob. "The Problem of the Wilderness," *Scientific Monthly*, February 1930. *"One looks from outside at works of art and architecture, listens from outside to music or poetry. But when one looks at and listens to the wilderness he is encompassed by his experience of beauty, lives in the midst of his esthetic universe . . . [we] fight for the freedom of free wilderness."*
- New York–New Jersey Trail Conference. *The Trail Conference publishes several hiking guides with detailed descriptions and excellent maps of hiking trails on both sides of the Hudson and beyond. See www.nynjtc.org/catalog/books to order books.*
- Rajs, Jake. *The Hudson River*. New York: The Monacelli Press, 1995. Spectacular color photographs of the Hudson River.

- Stanne, Stephen P.; Roger G. Panetta; Brian E. Forist. *The Hudson: An Illustrated Guide to the Living River.* New Brunswick, NJ: Rutgers University Press, 1996. A project of the Hudson River Sloop *Clearwater.* Educational, well-written, informative guide to habitats, fishes, and transformations along the Hudson.
- Thoreau, Henry. "Walking" in *Walden and Other Writings.* New York: Random House, 1937. *"A word for absolute freedom as contrasted with a freedom and culture merely civil to regard man as an inhabitant, or a part and parcel of nature. . . . Civilization needs wilderness to keep its strength and proper perspective . . . in wilderness is the preservation of the world."*

ENVIRONMENTAL, HIKING, AND OTHER GOOD HUDSON RIVER GROUPS

- Adirondack Mountain Club, www.adk.org
- Albany Institute of History and Art, 125 Washington Avenue Albany, www.albanyinstitute.org
- American Littoral Society, www.littoralsociety.org
- Appalachian Mountain Club, NY/NJ Chapter, www.amc-ny.org
- Audubon Society of New York State, http://ny.audubon.org
- Auto-Free New York/Transportation Alternatives, http://transalt.org
- Bergen Save the Watershed Action Network, www.bergenswan.org
- Brooklyn Botanic Garden, 1000 Washington Avenue Brooklyn, www.bbg.org
- Catskill Center for Conservation and Development, 43355 State Route 28, Arkville, www.catskillcenter.org
- Coalition for the Bight, 121 6th Ave., Ste. 501, NYC
- Council on the Environment of New York City, www.grownyc.org
- Environmental Planning Lobby/EPL-Environmental Advocates, www.envadvocates.org
- Federation to Preserve the Greenwich Village Waterfront and Great Port, Inc., 156 Perry Street, NYC
- Friends of the Shawangunks, http://shawangunks.org
- Gaia Institute, www.gaiainstituteny.org
- Garrison Landing Association, Dock House, Garrison
- Heritage Task Force for the Hudson River Valley, 21 South Putt Corners Rd., New Paltz
- Historic Hudson Valley, www.hudsonvalley.org
- Hudson River Environmental Society, www.hres.org/joomla

- Hudson River Foundation, www.hudsonriver.org/
- Hudson River Heritage, http://hudsonriverheritage.org
- Hudson River Maritime Museum, 50 Rondout Landing, Kingston, www.hrmm.org
- Hudson River Museum, 511 Warburton Avenue, Yonkers, www.hrm.org
- Hudson River National Estuarine Research Reserve, http://hrnerr.org
- Hudson River Park Conservancy, www.hudsonriverpark.org
- Hudson River Sloop *Clearwater,* www.clearwater.org
- Hudson River Valley Greenway Council, www.hudsongreenway.state.ny.us/Organization/GreenwayCouncil.aspx
- Hudsonia Limited, http://hudsonia.org
- Izaak Walton League of America, www.iwla.org
- Metropolitan Canoe & Kayak Club, PO Box 021868, Brooklyn, NY 11202-0400
- Metropolitan Waterfront Alliance, www.waterfrontalliance.org/
- NATURE, Pace University Environmental Center, 861 Bedford Road, Pleasantville
- The Nature Conservancy, Lower Hudson Chapter, 223 Katonah Avenue, Katonah, www.nature.org
- Neighborhood Open Space Coalition, 71 W 23rd Street, NYC 10010
- New York City Audubon Society, www.nycaudubon.org
- New York City Parks Department Central Park Arsenal, 5th Avenue, NYC, www.nycgovparks.org/parks/MT02
- New Yorkers for Parks, www.ny4p.org/
- NewYork/New Jersey Harbor Baykeeper, www.nynjbaykeeper.org
- New York–New Jersey Trail Conference, www.nynjtc.org
- New York Parks and Conservation Association, www.nypca.org
- New York Public Interest Research Group, www.nypirg.org
- New York State Department of Environmental Conservation, www.dec.ny.gov
- New York State, Department of State, www.dos.state.ny.us/
- New York State Office of Parks, Recreation, and Historic Preservation, http://nysparks.com/
- New York Turtle and Tortoise Society, http://nytts.org
- Open Space Institute, www.osiny.org
- Outdoors Club, Inc., www.outdoorsclubny.org
- Palisades Interstate Park Commission, www.njpalisades.org/pipc.htm
- Parks Council, 457 Madison Avenue, NYC

- Piermont Civic Association, PO Box 454, Piermont, www.piermont-ny.com/newsletter
- Protectors of Pine Oak Woods, www.siprotectors.org
- River Project, www.riverproject.org
- Riverside Park Fund, www.riversideparkfund.org
- Scenic Hudson, www.scenichudson.org
- Shorewalkers, PO Box 20748 Cathedral Station, NYC, http://shorewalkers.org
- Sierra Club, Atlantic Chapter, http://newyork.sierraclub.org
- Sierra Club, Hudson Mohawk Group, http://newyork.sierraclub.org/hudsonmohawk/index.html
- Sierra Club, Lower Hudson Group, http://newyork.sierraclub.org/LHG/
- Trust for Public Land, Mid-Atlantic Regional Office, www.tpl.org
- Wave Hill Environmental Center, West 249th Street, Bronx, http://wavehill.org

INDEX